A Search for God
BOOKS I & II

50th Anniversary Edition

A Search for God
BOOK I

1942

Compiled by Study Group #1 of the

Association for Research and Enlightenment, Inc.

Virginia Beach, Virginia

Table of Contents, Book I

Table of Contents, Book II

INTRODUCTION

This book changes lives.

Since 1931, individuals have been meeting to discuss, debate, and apply the material contained in this volume. Since that time literally thousands of groups (and tens of thousands of individuals) have found answers to questions that they sometimes could not even formulate. The information has positively affected lives worldwide.

A Search for God, Books I and II, were written to be helpful to individuals from all walks of life and all religious backgrounds. Whether a person comes from a Christian, Jewish, agnostic, or Eastern background, these books could reach out with the hope that true spirituality supersedes religious denomination. Admittedly, the group members responsible for this material presented their understanding of universal laws in what may appear to be decidedly "Christian" terminology. Their primary intent, however, was to explore the oneness of all life and the truths found in the wisdom of the world's religions. The lessons making up this material led the original group through a study of meditation, psychic ability, reincarnation, and universal laws—information that somehow bridged religious differences and found a common spirituality for all souls who are children of the same God. There are no claims to any unique revelation; in fact, a portion of the Preface states: "There is nothing new here. The search for God is as old as humanity."

Today, individuals from every religious tradition can be found in *Search for God* study groups the world over. These groups are ecumenical, yet, as we read and apply this material, it's important to remember that many of us may have biases and presupposed definitions about certain terms. Occasionally we may discover that they are not shared by others nor in line with the Cayce information itself. One key to working with *A Search for God* is to be open to the concepts and insights of others, and not become frustrated by the terminology used by a group of individuals who, more than fifty years ago, stated their insights in a language they could best understand.

The origins of *A Search for God* deserve special attention. In September, 1931, a group of ordinary people had a meeting with Edgar Cayce, one of the world's most notable clairvoyants and mystics. The meeting was called because the members wanted a new challenge. For several months they had been studying the great religious traditions of the world. Now they wanted to work more directly with Cayce's psychic information. Some wanted to become more spiritual; others, to know if they, like Edgar Cayce, could develop psychic abilities; a few others desired to be of service to a troubled world. But all members of the group hoped to discover more meaning and purpose in their lives.

In the first psychic reading to the group, Cayce offered a promise: if they were sincere in their desire and commitment, they could give "light to the waiting world." The group members made a covenant with one another and promised to follow certain disciplines to enhance their work together:

• They would meditate every morning in their own homes, conscious of the fact that the other group members were meditating at the same time.

• They would faithfully attempt to apply these lessons on spiritual laws suggested by Cayce's psychic information, share their own discoveries about the material with one another, and be attentive to insights and inspirations that came to them individually in meditation.

• They would submit questions about their own progress as well as questions on the lesson material to Cayce's psychic source.

• They would attempt to *live* what was being studied and to record their personal experiences for possible inclusion in the text they would write.

• They would not move on to the next lesson until each individual in the group had learned, understood, and applied the lesson being studied.

This final pledge led the group into an extraordinary commitment of time and energy. The series of twenty-four lessons outlined by Edgar Cayce took the group *eleven years* to apply and compile! Each lesson required an instructive essay that combined a summary of key principles along with brief reports on how group members had worked with the material.

Cayce's promise that the group could become a "light to the waiting world" was fulfilled. Study Group #1—as they called themselves—went on to author this book, *A Search for God.* Although the first twelve lessons, comprising Book I, were not published until 1942—marking 1992 as the 50th anniversary of *A Search for God,* Book I—additional groups formed soon after the initial lessons could be mimeographed. The remaining twelve lessons, comprising Book II, were finally published in 1950. This present special edition of Study Group #1's creation is the first time both books have been printed in one volume.

The lessons, given in sequential order, begin with "Cooperation." Although not part of the original series, a twenty-fifth lesson on "Meditation" was later added to give insights into Cayce's approach to this important discipline. According to Cayce's instructions, it was placed in the beginning of Book I.

Working creatively with *A Search for God* is much more than simply gaining knowledge of spiritual principles. Instead, this material must be applied, understood, and even "lived" so that we can move beyond mere intellectual knowledge about concepts into a true *awareness* of universal laws operating in our daily lives. When *A Search for God* is approached from this perspective, it can truly facilitate lasting, meaningful, personal change. In fact, these twenty-four lessons have been called one of the earliest and most effective tools for group therapy and personal transformation introduced in the Western Hemisphere.

Interestingly, in 1934 a Cayce reading told Study Group #1 that the life-changing insights of their experiences would still be helping people a hundred years into the future. Today, nearly sixty years later, that prediction is clearly being realized. You, too, can become a part of that promise. To find out where *A Search for God* study group meets near you, contact:

A.R.E.
215 67th Street
Virginia Beach, VA 23451-2061

Few teachings about the spiritual path have stood the test of time. This edition, *A Search for God,* is one of them.

NOTE:

Numbers at the end of quotes are file numbers of psychic readings by Edgar Cayce. The original readings are in the custody of the Edgar Cayce Foundation, Virginia Beach, Va.

Bible references are taken from the King James Version.

P.E. refers to a personal experience.

P.R. refers to a psychic reading.

In some instances in the text of this edition, nouns and pronouns have been modified from the male gender to be inclusive of both genders, i.e., *mankind* to **humankind.**

PREFACE

Try living the precepts of this book.

Here is a unique compilation of information dealing with spiritual laws of daily living. Why is it unique?

The manuscript resulted from the study and work of the original Study Group #1 of the Association for Research and Enlightenment, Incorporated, Virginia Beach, Virginia. It was written not by one person but by many individuals.

The affirmations and basic discourses under each chapter heading came from general readings given by Edgar Cayce. Questions were asked and experiences during meditation explained in subsequent readings for twelve people.

To these individuals it brought hope, peace, a better understanding of their fellow human beings and an inner joy in a greater awareness of attunement with the Creator.

There is nothing new here. The search for God is as old as humanity. This book is passed on in the hope that through it, during the trying times ahead, many may glimpse a ray of light; that in other hearts it may awaken a new hope and vision of a better world through application of His laws in daily life.

aa parallel

Prayer

Our Father which art in HEAVEN,
  Hallowed be thy NAME.
Thy kingdom come. Thy WILL be done in earth,
  as it is in heaven.
Give us this day our daily BREAD.
And forgive us our DEBTS, as we forgive
  our debtors.
And lead us not into TEMPTATION,
  but deliver us from EVIL:
For thine is the KINGDOM, and the POWER,
  and the GLORY, for ever. Amen.

Matthew 6:9-13

MEDITATION

The Edgar Cayce readings repeatedly emphasized the importance of meditation as an integral ingredient for personal transformation. In fact, they suggested that the following information on "Meditation" be added to the twenty-four lessons that comprise A Search for God. However, to become familiar with the group process, some readers may wish to start with the chapter on "Cooperation," reading the meditation information individually or picking it up later for group discussion.

I. Introduction

In this material world we are conscious of the phenomenon of growth. We should be equally aware of spiritual progression that includes both a broadening of understanding of the relation between the Creator and ourselves, and a definite improvement in capacities for more useful lives. Too much stress has been placed upon the desirability of escaping from physical existence. The average individual has come to look upon spiritual things as being intangible and ethereal, unconnected with normal life.

The eternal question that runs through life is this: What is truly valuable in thought, in activity, and in experience? Only from within can come a stable estimate of what is worthwhile. This sense of appreciation or this inner realization is based fundamentally upon an understanding of self—self in relation to others and self in relation to God. Meditation is the means to this end.

II. Prayer and Meditation

1. Prayer defined and illustrated

Some individuals give little thought to either prayer or meditation. They are satisfied to drift with the current, hoping that somehow or somewhere conditions will work out for the best for them. There are others who seek a better way, searching for that light which renews hope, gives a more perfect understanding of their present lot, and justifies the course of life that is being pursued.

Prayer is the concerted effort of our physical consciousnesses to become attuned to the Consciousness of the Creator. It is the attunement of our conscious minds to the spiritual forces that manifest in a material world. It may be a cooperative experience of many individuals, coming together with one accord and with one mind.

Prayer to some is the pouring out of personality for outward show, to be seen by others. To others it means entering into the closet of the inner self and pouring out the ego so that the inner being may be filled with the Spirit of the Father. These divergent attitudes are illustrated in the example drawn by Christ.

> "Two men went up into the temple to pray, the one a Pharisee, and the other a publican. The Pharisee stood and prayed thus with himself, God, I thank thee, that I am not as other men are, extortioners, unjust, adulterers, or even as this publican. I fast twice in the week, I give tithes of all that I possess. And the publican, standing afar off, would not lift up so much as his eyes unto heaven, but smote upon his breast, saying, God be merciful to me a sinner. I tell you, [said Jesus] this man went down to his house justified rather than the other." *Luke 18:10-14*

2. Meditation defined

Meditation is the emptying of ourselves of all that hinders the Creative Force from rising along the natural channels of our physical bodies to be disseminated through the sensitive spiritual centers in our physical bodies. When meditation is properly entered into, we are made stronger mentally and physically. "He went in the strength of that meat received for many days." (281-13)

Meditation is not musing or daydreaming, but attuning our mental and physical bodies to their spiritual source. It is arousing the mental and spiritual attributes to an expression of their relationship with their Maker. This is true meditation.

Meditation is prayer from within the inner self and partakes not only of the inner physical person but of the soul aroused by the spirit from within. In prayer we speak to God, in meditation God speaks to us.

3. Will prayer answer for meditation?

Will asking a question answer it? No, but it shows that we desire information, and therefore it has its merits. Just so when we pray. We show to our heavenly Father that we are anxious for His guidance and help, for the manifestation of His promises in our lives. It then takes an attitude of waiting, of silence, of listening, to be able to hear the still small voice whisper within, and to know that all is well. Prayer therefore is the basis of meditation.

Only when we are still may we know God, and when we know Him we are willing to say and mean, "Thy will be done." It is then that He sups with us.

In prayer we ask for cleansing; before true meditation we must be clean in body and mind so that we may be fit to meet our Lord. One is a complement of the other.

III. Preparation for Meditation

A. *The Physical Body*

1. A knowledge, cleansing, and consecration of the physical body

We are miniature copies of the universe, possessing physical, mental, and spiritual bodies. These bodies are so closely knit together that the impressions of one have their effects upon the other two. The physical body is a composite unit of creative force manifesting in a material world. So all-inclusive is the physical body that there is nothing in the universe that we can comprehend that does not have its miniature replica within it. It is not only our privilege but our duty to know ourselves, and to be aware of our bodies being temples of the living God.

Individuals have found throughout the ages that preparation is necessary for deep meditation. For some it is necessary that the body be cleansed with pure water, that certain foods or associations (with man or woman) be avoided, and that certain types of breathing be taken so that there may be an even balance in the whole respiratory system. This produces a normal flow of circulation through the body. Others feel that odors, incantations, sounds, or music are conducive to producing the best conditions. As the current rises through the centers in the body, these outer influences may help to cleanse the thoughts and quiet the mind and body. So-called savages arouse within themselves the passions or thirst for destruction through the battle cry or the use of certain drones or sounds. This is the same force used negatively. (See 440-12 and 281-13.)

The following is an illustration: An engineer, before going into an electric power plant for work, must take off a certain type of wearing apparel and put on another. His mind must be filled with a thorough knowledge and understanding of the mechanism to be handled, lest death and destruction result. How much more is a cleansing and understanding necessary when we seek to attune our bodies to the source of all force? He has promised to meet us within our own sanctuary. One that goes in unworthily does it to one's own destruction.

While the method may not be the same with everyone, if we would meditate, we must shut ourselves away from the cares of the world and purify our bodies physically. "Consecrate yourselves this day," is given in the law, "that ye may on the morrow present yourselves before the Lord that He may speak through *you!*" (281-13) as a father speaketh with his children. Have we wandered so far away that we dare not await His presence? Do we not remember He has promised "If ye will be my children I will be your God" and "Though ye wander far away, if ye will but call I will hear"? (281-41)

We must find that which to our consciousness is the best way of purifying body and mind before attempting to enter into meditation. In raising the image of that through which we are seeking to know the will of the Creative Force, actual creation takes place within us.

When we have found a way to cleanse our bodies so that which is to be raised finds its full measure of expression within, we can readily understand how healing of every nature may be disseminated by thought.

When we have cleansed ourselves in the manner that is to us the best, there will be no fear that our experiences will become so overpowering as to cause any physical or mental disorder. It is when there is no cleansing that entering into such a state brings disaster, or pain, or disease.

2. A study of the glands

When we quiet the physical body through turning the mind toward the highest ideal, there are aroused actual physical vibrations, as a result of spiritual influence becoming active on the sensitive vibratory centers in the body, stimulating the points of contact between the soul and its physical shell. Let us trace this activity.

When we attune ourselves to the Infinite, the glands of reproduction may be compared to a motor which raises the spiritual power in the body. This spiritual power enters through the center of the cells of Leydig glands (located in the genitive system). This center is like a sealed or open door, according to the use to which it has been put through spiritual activities. With the arousing of the image, or ideal, this life force rises along what is known as the Appian Way or the silver cord, to the pineal center in the brain, whence it may be disseminated to those centers that give activity to the whole mental and physical being. It rises then to the hidden eye in the center of the brain system (pituitary body), which is just back of the middle of the forehead. Thus on entering meditation there arises a definite impulse from the glands of reproduction that passes through the pineal to the pituitary gland. Whatever the ideal of an individual is, it is propelled upward and finds expression in the activity of the imaginative forces. If this ideal is material, there is built more and more into the body a love for, and a tendency towards, things of the earth. If this ideal or image is of a spiritual nature there is spiritual development. Psychic forces are only an awakening of soul faculties through activities in these centers. If an anatomical or pathological study should be made for a period of seven years (which is the cycle of change in all body elements), of an individual who is acted upon through the pituitary gland alone, it would be discovered that such a person trained in spiritual laws would become a light to the world. One trained in purely material things would become a Frankenstein [monster], without a concept of any influence other than material or mental. (See 262-20.)

During the rising of the currents along this silver cord and in these centers, a body may become conscious of distinct vibrations. There are three principal motions that correspond to the three-dimensional concept of the conscious mind: namely, the backward

and forward, the side to side, and the circular movements. These
sensations may be very real. They may cause an apparent
vibration or motion in the body itself that is simply a movement
within the body, without outward effect. Another very common
sensation is that of the current or vibration passing up the spine
or through the body from the feet upward, or vice versa. These
may also be accompanied or followed by a lightness, or slight
dizziness. It may also be pointed out here that the reactions
within individuals may differ, for the composite vibrations of a
body acted upon by spiritual thought differ in various individuals.
The important point is that a definite, physical reaction, in
sensitive centers, takes place.

3. A study of vibrations

Before entering further into the discussion of meditation, it
would be well to outline a few elementary principles of vibration
which will enable us to better understand many of the terms
used, and some of the experiences we may have. Science teaches
us that all matter is in motion, and that the difference in various
forms of matter is due to the difference in the rates of vibration.
For example, we know that by increasing the molecular activity
of water by heating we can produce another form of matter called
steam; that is, the particles of matter in the steam are vibrating
(moving) at a faster rate of speed than the particles in water.
Now, our bodies are made up of particles of matter which have
been taken into them, such as food, air, et cetera. Various parts
of our bodies are composed of different types of matter, vibrating
at different rates of speed. The nervous system, for example, is
highly sensitive. Our bones are of denser structure than our
blood, muscular tissue denser than membrane, and so on. The
combination of the vibrations of all of these different parts forms
a general rate of vibration for the body. This is constantly
changing. Illness of any kind causes discordant vibrations. The
higher the rate of vibration, the more sensitive the body is to
influences of any kind.

As we go deeper in the study of meditation, we become
conscious, through application, of these various vibrations in
and through the body and mind. As we attempt deep meditation,
spiritual forces within and without the body-mind will at first be
limited by the five senses of perception, for only through these

can we recognize any manifestation in this plane. Even when we have learned to lay the physical aside entirely and explore wider realms, the concepts brought back with us must be clothed in three-dimensional terms to be consciously understood.

Vibrations which are emanations of life from within are material expressions of a spiritual influence, a force that emanates from life itself. When a vibration arises, it may act only upon centers within the human body that are sensitive to vibrations, else they may not become apparent. These, spiritualized, are emanations which may be sent out as thought waves, as a force in the activity of universal or cosmic influence, and thus have their effect upon those toward whom, by suggestion, they are directed. (See 281-7 and 281-12.)

Let us consider the effect of thought upon the body in relation to vibration. All thoughts are constructed at different vibratory rates. As the food we take into the body is important from the standpoint of structure, so thoughts are important as factors that build up the mental pattern. Mind is the builder. It is the construction engineer that molds even the actual physical matter in its higher vibratory forms. We should therefore never use thought vibrations by attempting to make ourselves other than a channel to help others.

B. *The Mental Body*

1. The purging of self

Let us consider what takes place in the mental body during meditation. The mind is the builder, the physical the result. The mind partakes of both the physical and the spiritual. Most of us are aware of only a part of the mind; this we call the conscious mind. Even in the field of psychology, recent investigations have revealed little beyond a bare glance at what is called the subconscious, the storehouse of memory and the ever-watchful supervisor of the regular functions of the body. There is still another division of the mind. This may be called the activity of the superconscious, or soul-mind. (These are only names that we use in trying to clarify for our imperfect understanding the meanings of different functions of one force.)

Through meditation we seek to allow our mind to function normally. Through the will we ask the mind of our physical bodies to cease its wanderings and center itself upon the ideal, which will be presented to the higher mind. This ideal becomes the basis for the activity which results.

If the ideal and purpose we hold are in accord with the superconscious mind, that which will be of help and value to the physical mind and body will be transmitted into consciousness through some channel of the five senses. Proof of this higher mental activity will come to each of us as we seek to understand. If, however, the ideal and purpose are out of harmony with the soul-mind, the opening of the door between the physical and spiritual will result in turmoil within, striking at the weakest point.

So it is necessary to purify our minds if we would meditate. Think of what we should do to have our God meet us face to face. Would we say, "Many are not able to speak to God, many are fearful"? (281-41) Have we gone so far astray that we cannot approach Him who is all-merciful? He knows our desires and needs, yet He can supply us only according to the purposes within ourselves.

Then let us purify our bodies, our minds, and consecrate ourselves in prayer. Let us put away from us hate, greed, and malice, and replace them with love and mercy. Let there be in our hearts humbleness, for we must humble ourselves if we would know Him. Let us come with an open, seeking, contrite heart desiring to have the way shown us. Then let us seek to enter.

2. The attunement of self to the Whole

Attunement depends upon soul development. Physically, the radio may be an illustration. The attunement on any radio may be somewhere near the same point of another, but on no two, even when sitting side by side, will it be the same, for the position of the sets alters that. So in attuning our consciousness to the Divine, each of us must make the attunement according to our own development. Attunement, like all attainments in creation, is a growth. "In my Father's house are many mansions [states of consciousness] . . . I go and prepare a place for you...that where I am [in consciousness], there ye may be also [in consciousness]."[1]

Proper attunement is necessary for true meditation. A perfect attunement may be made with the Ideal, the Infinite, when we make our minds and our wills one with His in word, action, intent, and purpose. Let us pray, "Father, not my will but Thine

[1]John 14:2, 3

be done in and through me," (262-3) and mean it.

How may we know we are not in attunement? It is when we have lost interest in our fellow human beings. To be out of harmony with our neighbor is to be out of harmony with our Maker. Does not the Bible say, "If thou bring thy gift to the altar, and there remembereth that thy brother hath ought against thee; Leave there thy gift before the altar, and go thy way; first be reconciled to thy brother, and then come and offer thy gift."[2] "Thou shalt love the Lord thy God with all thy heart . . . and thy neighbour as thyself."[3]

C. *The Spiritual Body*

1. The soul

It is through meditation that we may become aware of the existence of the spiritual forces within, that we unlock the door between our physical and spiritual bodies. Through this door come impulses from the soul, seeking expression in the physical.

Our souls are endowed with many faculties that are limited and bound by our impressions in the physical. The soul is always present, always willing to express its true purpose, its true relationship with the Creator. Through meditation we make this possible; we open the way.

Some say that we are not conscious of possessing a soul. We should know that each of us is a soul. This body in which we live is only our house for the moment, and then out of it we go on to other states of consciousness and other experiences.

The fact that we hope, that we have desires for better things, that we are able to be sorry or glad, indicates activities of the mind that take hold upon something that is not temporal in nature, something that does not pass away at the death of the body. Such mental activities come from the spiritual center of our being, the soul. God breathed the breath of life into Adam and he became a living soul.[4]

Then, each is a soul endowed with the attributes of God, possessing the power of creation, of being one with the Father, a joint heir with the Son. We are made in His image

2. The ideal

There are as many types of meditation as there are individuals who meditate. For some it is an escape from the trials of the

[2]Matt. 5:23, 24   [3]Luke 10:27   [4]See Genesis 2:7

world; for others it is an access to knowledge; for still others it is an approach to God. Various forms of meditation exist, each with its adherents. But the real significance is in the ideal and purpose. The sweetest incense or the most beautiful music will not lift a selfish heart into the presence of the Creator. It is much more important that our minds be free of malice, hate, greed, and selfishness, than that some complex form for meditation be observed. Let us not become involved and confused by material means to meditation, but rather consider first the fundamental reason for it and make that reason in harmony with the highest desire we can conceive.

There are definite changes that take place within us when we enter into true or deep meditation. There is physical activity, through the imaginative or impulsive powers. The sources of impulse are aroused by shutting out thoughts pertaining to activities or attributes of carnal forces. Changes naturally take place when there is an arousing of those stimuli within us which have the seat of the soul as a home. If the ideal, the image, the mark of a high calling, is a standard which is in accord with the highest aspiration of service which we can recognize, then we bear the mark of the Lamb, the Christ. As we raise this, we are able to enter into the very presence of the Creative Force. (See 281-13.)

Some of us have so overshadowed ourselves by abuses of the mental attributes of the body that only an imperfect image may be raised within.

If our aims of meditation are only to still the physical, the direct method should be used. But this is not usually the case. A higher state of spiritual consciousness is the aim and purpose of deep meditation. It is important, therefore, that attention be fixed upon the ideal which is to be raised. The physical quiet of the human organism will follow as a natural result, and there will be a growth of unity, of inner feeling, rather than separate, broken points of consciousness. Now, in fixing attention upon the ideal there should be created a desire to reach the highest possible state of awareness of which the whole being is capable. This does not mean fixation upon the words of an affirmation, but a strong desire that the meeting with the inner self and God be unobstructed and unmarred by other distractions. The quieting of the body should result from an inner spiritual effort rather than from a fixation of consciousness on outer stimuli.

IV. The Forces

In meditation, more than at any other time, we become conscious of the forces. We refer to them as psychic, occult, intuitive, universal, and so on. These are only names designating the various functions of God. "Hear, O Israel: the Lord our God is one Lord."[5]

Let us consider, for an example, intuitive force that arises from experiences of our whole being. It can be developed by introspective activities of our conscious mind, until it is able to bring to bear such experiences upon our daily lives. We call this "entering into the silence."[6]

Those who by constant introspection are able to bring to the surface their experiences as a whole are called "sages" or "lamas." When this ability is made practical by an individual and yet remains spiritual in aspect, such an individual becomes a master.

There is much to be gained in the study of the forces through meditation, introspection, or entering into the silence. It is well to have a thorough knowledge of the subject, but never pretend to be mysterious about it. Jesus lived simply, doing good among His fellow human beings.

As we, in meditation, open ourselves to the unseen forces that surround the throne of grace, beauty, and might within ourselves, let us throw around us the protection found in the thought of the Christ. When our minds are on God, the Christ, who is our Ideal, we need not worry about destructive results. Remember the promise, "Behold, I stand at the door, and knock: if any man hear my voice, and open the door, I will come in to him, and will sup with him, and he with me."[7] "It is I; be not afraid."[8]

It is when we hold the right ideal that our problems are solved and stumbling blocks become stepping-stones.

V. Methods of Meditation

We must learn to meditate just as we learn to walk or talk or to develop any physical attribute.

We must direct our consciousness through desire, controlled by will.

[5]Deut. 6:4   [6]P.R.   [7]Rev. 3:20   [8]Matt. 14:27

The following suggestions are offered as an outline that may be used by each individual. We are all capable of choosing the form that is most pleasing, most suitable, and most fitting for us as individuals. Our various developments fit us to accept and understand different forms. For some, the simplest approach is the best; for others, a complicated procedure is necessary. There must be a spiritual intent and purpose, a true desire to seek His will, not ours, as we enter in. God is spiritual force and must be sought through a spiritual ideal, set by Him who perfected the way, and who thus became the Way. Let His principles be the guide in the formation of the ideal, the image, that is raised within.

Cleanse the body with pure water. Sit or lie in an easy position, without binding garments about the body. Three times breathe in through the right nostril and exhale through the mouth; three times breathe in through the left nostril and exhale through the right nostril. Then, either with the aid of low music or an incantation which carries the self deeper into a sense of oneness with the creative forces of love, enter into the Holy of Holies. As self feels or experiences the raising of this, see it disseminated through the inner eye (not carnal eye) to that which will bring the greater understanding in meeting every condition in the experience of the body. Then, we may listen to the music that is made as each center of the body responds to the new Creative Force that is being disseminated, each through its own channel. We will find that, little by little, meditation will enable us to renew ourselves physically, mentally, and spiritually. (See 281-28.)

Experiences

1. In meditation some individuals experience a vibratory sensation which seems to move the body from side to side, or backward and forward. This may become a circular motion within the body, bringing a fullness and whirling sensation in the head.

2. Other individuals feel a coolness upon the head and forehead.

3. Some sense a pulsation in the lower part of the spine. This may come from nerve impulses flowing through the body from the lower genitive centers to other gland centers which control various activities of the physical body. Let us not force these, but so conduct our minds and the activities of our bodies as to leave

ourselves channels for such expressions.

4. Others experience a vibration running up through the body and ending in a sensation of fullness in the head. When we are able to raise within ourselves vibrations that pass through the whole course of the attributes of physical attunements to the disseminating center, or spiritual eye, then our bodies become magnets that may, if properly used, bring healing to others, with a laying on of hands.

5. A sensation to the eyes is indicative of a healing vibration. Healing of every sort must come first in self before it can be raised in another.

6. A voice speaking to an individual is a manifestation of an awakening within self of the abilities to associate, connect, and communicate with those influences from without self. Then, as given of old, if there will be held and magnified within the consciousness of self the desire for that Voice, that Presence, which would aid in bringing the various consciousnesses to self, the experiences will be from the universal influences or from His messenger. Magnify this in self and for self. Be mindful that it is not clothed in some other power.

7. Then, finally, there is the passing into the presence of that which may materialize in voice, feeling, sight, and a consciousness of oneness with the Whole.

VI. Conclusion

If self-development is our aim, then we must begin just where we are. It will do no good idly to wish to be in some other condition or surrounding; for, unless we have mastered our present state, the second will be worse than the first. The first and last obstacle to overcome is understanding ourselves. Until we are fully aware of all that constitutes our existence we have no right to say that this or that is the aim and goal of life. Our capacities and abilities are of the highest creation. Let us not fool ourselves by accepting anything but the fullest expression of consciousness.

Meditation is the safest and surest way to understand ourselves. It is the key to the door which is closed on the real world for most of us. Let us study and know ourselves. It is a command, an entreaty. Let us dare to seek, not blindly, but with faith, that we may find "the noble self." (See 281-7.) Our approaches and

I have had such a strong sense of
bom of those. I feel divinely compelled -9/11/13

14   A SEARCH FOR GOD

results may differ, but the same understanding, the same point of consciousness, and the same state of awareness are the ultimate goals. Two attitudes are essential:

1. A strong desire to seek truth.
2. A constant, consistent effort to move forward.

WORK, WORK, WORK

Let us be continuous and regular in meditation. Broken periods of meditation will accomplish little. Be active in holding the ideal, and be regular in awakening the inner self.

In the end, the reward is well worth the effort expended. Most of us waste hours each day when just a few moments spent in daily search within would bring more peace and joy, and more true happiness, than any physical activity. Then let us first seek the kingdom of heaven. Where is the kingdom of heaven? It is within. What He gave of old is as true today as it was in the beginning. Let us call on Him and know that our bodies are temples of the living God. There He has promised to meet us.

Are we afraid? Are we ashamed? Have we so belittled our opportunities, have we so defamed our own bodies and our own minds that we are ashamed to have our God meet us within our tabernacles? If such is the case, let us set our houses in order.

There are spiritual centers in our bodies which are points of physical contact between the physical organism and the soul. These connections are just as real as the nerve centers and fibers which carry impulses from one of the sense organs to the brain. There is a bowl that must one day be broken, and a cord that must one day be severed from the physical body of each individual.[9] The ultimate goal of each soul's searching is a greater awareness of God. Through meditation we may increase this awareness in daily life and prepare the way for the change called death to bring us another step forward toward the goal.

What is our God? Are we ambitious only as to whether we shall eat tomorrow or as to wherewithal we shall be clothed? We are of little faith and of little hope who allow such to become the paramount issues in our consciousness. Know we not that we are His? We are of His making. He has willed that we shall not perish, but has left it with us as to whether we become even aware of our relationships with Him. In our houses, our bodies, there are ways for the approach—through the desire to know Him. We put that desire into activity by purging our bodies and

[9]See Eccles. 12:6

our minds of those things that we know, or even conceive of, as being hindrances. It has been given of old that it was not for those who would descend from heaven to bring us a message, or those who would come from over the seas, but that we would find Him within our own hearts and consciousnesses.

Would we ask God to do for us what we would not do for our neighbor? If we would, we are selfish and cannot know God, for as we do it unto the least of our brethren, we do it unto our Maker. These are not mere words—they can be experiences, if we seek to know Him. He is not past finding out. If we would know Him, we must turn to Him; look, hope, and act in such a way that we expect Him, our God, to meet us face to face. "It is I; be not afraid,"[10] said He who came to those seeking to know their relationship with their Maker.

Many of us become afraid because of the things that we hear, and we say, "I do not understand, I do not comprehend." Why? Have we so belittled ourselves, our bodies, our minds, and our consciousnesses that we have seared and made of no effect those opportunities within us to know our Maker?

Let us purify our bodies and our minds. Let us consecrate ourselves in prayer. Let there be humbleness in our hearts, for we must humble ourselves if we would know Him, and come with an open, seeking, contrite spirit, desirous of having the way shown to us.

When we are shown the way, let us not turn away, but be true to the vision that is given us. He will speak, for His promise has been "When ye call I will hear and will answer speedily."[11] Then when He speaks, let us open our hearts and our minds to the opportunities and glories that are ours. We can accept them through attuning our consciousnesses to the Christ Consciousness in meditation. Then we can say and mean it, "Let others do as they may, but as for us, we will worship—yea, we will serve—the living God."[12]

Even in those times of greatest trial He is not far from us. He is closer than our right hand. He stands at the door of our hearts. Will we bid Him enter, or will we turn Him away? (See 281-41.)

[10]Matt. 14:27   [11]P.R. See Psalm 102:2   [12]P.R. See Joshua 24:15

Lesson I

COOPERATION

"Finally, be ye all of one mind, having compassion one of another; love as brethren."   I Peter 3:8

Step 3.

Affirmation

Not my will but Thine, O Lord, be done in me and through me. Let me ever be a channel of blessings, today, now, to those that I contact in every way. Let my going in, my coming out be in accord with that Thou would have me do, and as the call comes, "Here am I, send me, use me."   *262-3*

Reminds me of St. Francis prayer

12th Step work

I

COOPERATION

[Based on Edgar Cayce readings 262-1 through 262-5]

Introduction

Cooperation in the physical is defined as acting or operating jointly with others, concurring with others in action or effort. In the spiritual it is more. It is losing sight of self and becoming a channel through which blessings may flow to others. The blessing is cooperation in action. Whether in the spiritual or physical, action is necessary to put cooperation into operation—thus those who would come together for a common cause must have united action in the pursuit and realization of a common end.

The best in life is ours, not at the expense of others, but in harmonious cooperation. In every successful organization the law is in effect. The heavens declare the Hand which formed them was the Hand of unity, order, and harmony. All nature follows the same law. Each part of the human body performs its duty without a thought of the other, yet fully depending each upon the other.

When self is lost in the Ideal, cooperation is the natural result. It is the natural consequence of self-service, self-sacrifice, self-bewilderment in Him.

In whatever state we find society, let us meet it upon its own level; as we look up, we lift it. That is cooperation.

law of attraction

Need for Cooperation

We must put cooperation into action in our thinking. Our adverse thoughts have such a paralyzing effect that they will not only retard our own development, but also will build barriers for

19

those who might seek to aid us. The Master could do no mighty works in His own village because of the people's unbelief in Him. Thoughts are deeds and may become crimes or miracles in their application. It is necessary for the accomplishment of any aim, for the reaching of any goal, and for the attainment of any blessing for self or humanity that we have one mind, one aim, and one purpose.

As we seek, in our way, to cooperate in being of service to others, we are lifted up. Let us, then, express the Creative Force within us in such a way that it may bring hope, peace, and understanding into the lives of others, that they too, in their way, may seek to be channels of blessings.

Then, let us attune ourselves to the highest spiritual Force. This will come when we are in accord with His will.

Let us exercise our conscious mind by holding these two thoughts before us:

1. We must lose ourselves in Him.

2. Our every thought and our every deed must be in harmony with the intent and purposes of the best that is within us.

What is the mind of the Christ that we should seek?

As we open our minds, our hearts, and our souls, that we may be channels of blessings, we then have the mind of the Christ, who took upon Himself the burden of the world. So may we, in our little spheres, take upon ourselves the burdens of our world. The joy, peace, and happiness that may be ours are found in doing for the other person. Gaining an understanding of the laws that pertain to right living in all its phases makes our minds in attune with Creative Forces. (See *A Search for God*, Book II, pp. 224-225.) We have the mind of Christ by putting into action that which we know.

Method of Obtaining Cooperation

Now, the questions arise: How may we accomplish this? How may we work as individuals whose purposes will be in accord with His will? To answer these we must look within to the little things that go to make up our very nature. We must guard our daily thoughts and acts, and must, through meditation, awaken our inner selves.

Step 10

In the daily walk of life let us take stock of our thoughts and acts, for cooperation is the offering of self to be a channel of activity, of thought. It is not attained at once, but comes line upon line, precept upon precept, through the giving of self. We must realize that they who would have life must give life; they who would have love must show themselves lovable; they who would have friends must be friendly; they who would have cooperation must cooperate by giving self to that which is to be accomplished, whether in bringing light, strength, health, or understanding to others. These are one in Him.

Let us replace our negative thoughts with positive ones, thinking not unkindly of anyone but speaking and thinking kindly of all. Let us practice thinking kind thoughts of those who have hurt us, letting no opportunity pass to do a little act of kindness that will lighten the burden of another. We should live as we know He would have us live. Begin now. Work! Work diligently and consistently. Let us take thought continually of the attitude of mind we hold; for it makes for that which gives birth to peace, harmony, and understanding; or it brings forth the contending forces that make for unrest and trouble. We will find, when we would do right, that the spirit of unrest is ever present; but day by day this should be put out of our minds and more and more replaced by thoughts of peace, harmony, and understanding—not a latent kind, but an active force. This is the manner in which we give expression to that being sought.

It is a oneness of mind, a oneness of purpose, which we must all seek; the virtue in the knowledge of God—His laws, His precepts—not to the advantage of self, but for others; not for self-edification, but that power and strength may emanate from us to others less strong. Let us seek harmony, for harmony makes for peace, and peace makes for understanding, and understanding for enlightenment.

We of ourselves can do nothing; so let us, in meditation, seek the knowledge of the inner Light. Set aside a time each day for prayer and meditation, preferably at sunrise; quiet the physical body, purify the emotions, and wait on the Lord. Let us draw nigh unto God and He will draw nigh unto us.

As we enter into meditation, let us visualize the force of harmony and love in action. As we put into practice that which we know of cooperation in deed and in thought, there will come to us His peace which passes understanding, and the realization of being His channel. He has promised that power, strength, joy, life, and light will not be withheld from those who seek this oneness in His name.

Realization of Cooperation

As the realization of a perfect cooperation in Him comes to us, there will come also the knowledge of our oneness with the Creative Force of the universe. Self-interest will be eliminated. Joy and happiness, found in service, will reign in our hearts. Our bodies and our minds will function more perfectly, because the Creative Force, which ever seeks expression in all, has been aroused in us. Understanding will come as quietly as the silent shadows of night, and His everlasting peace will live in our hearts.

There is perhaps no better way to illustrate this realization than to quote a few of the experiences of those who have sought light and understanding through cooperation.

"In experiencing cooperation I have been led into a greater field of spiritual understanding and realize that I am a channel through which His will may be done."

"I experienced in my trials a feeling of cooperation from our study group, in that through their prayers and meditations I realized that nothing but good could come to me. All fear was allayed. I knew that justice and mercy would prevail. There came to me a feeling of contentment, a willingness to leave all in His hands, and a realization that all was well."

"With the cooperation of our study group, I have been better able to understand my own individual purpose in relation to the whole purpose of life. At times, when our cooperation was greatest, I have been able to feel myself being a perfect channel through which God manifested. During the nights following such attunements, I have had visions and dreams that were testimonies to me of growth and development."

"I have realized that faithful repetition of efforts which make for cooperation brings at times a feeling of unity with all with whom I work, and a nearness of His presence, which shows that His promise, 'Where two or three are gathered together in My name, there am I in the midst of them,"[1] is sure."

"In my meditation I have seen our study group come together and form a complete circle, each member of the group being represented by a dot. Each one in the circle seemed to call the others by name and bless them. The circle now turned to a wheel, the dots becoming spokes. Each spoke represented a member of the group. Each spoke became a channel, leading outward from the hub, where was seen the Christ Light. As the blessings of love, harmony, peace, and understanding flowed from the Christ through the channels, the wheel was able to turn. This was cooperation in action. As the wheel revolved, members of the group or channels were able to turn other wheels, which were helping to bring the world to light, love, harmony, and true understanding."

These are the goals for each of us to reach in our varied experiences: unity of purpose, oneness of mind—in that His will, not ours, nor our personalities, may be manifested in all that we do and teach.

Let us be patient and untiring in seeking this cooperation, for we will be preparing ourselves to go on in the study and understanding of spiritual forces, and will become active channels for these higher forces. We will be better husbands, better wives, better neighbors, and better friends. The little world in which we live will be happier for our being a part of it. We will bring more joy and happiness to those about us and will be manifesting God's love for us.

The way is being opened for all who will to have a part in the redemption of humanity. We must keep our hearts singing, not in sorrow but in gladness of purpose, for of all those chosen of Him we should be the happiest. May our united efforts go through the ages to those yet unborn, regenerating them to that awakening which makes all souls safe in the knowledge of Him who made all things, for "without him was not any thing made that was made."[2]

> Not my will but Thine, O Lord, be done in me and through me. Let me ever be a channel of blessings, today, now, to those that I contact in every way. Let my going in, my coming out be in accord with that Thou would have me do, and as the call comes, "Here am I, send me, use me." *262-3*

Really great 3rd step prayer

[1]Matt. 18:20   [2]John 1:3

Lesson II

KNOW THYSELF

"Now ye are the body of Christ, and members in particular."
I Corinthians 12:27

Affirmation

Father, as we seek to see and know Thy face, may we each, as individuals and as a group, come to know ourselves, even as we are known, that we—as lights in Thee—may give the better concept of Thy Spirit in this world.   *262-5*

II

KNOW THYSELF

[Based on Edgar Cayce readings 262-5 through 262-11]

Introduction

When we are asked the question "Do you know yourself?" why is it that we cannot answer "Yes"? Within each of us there are certainly great storehouses of abilities and capacities which we have never used. If they were manifested, we would see ourselves in a different light. We would understand the real functions of our physical bodies in relation to our mental and spiritual bodies. Until we are better acquainted with ourselves, we are barriers in the way of our own development.

Each of us must first know that we must set a standard of measurement, of valuation, of precept, and of concept. Let us not measure by earthly standards, if we would know ourselves. Rather, let us measure by that which we have found within ourselves to be our ideal, knowing what we believe in, and acting that way. Let us, therefore, be willing to be measured; not by what we have, but by what we give.

The Physical Body

To know ourselves is not only to be cognizant of the acts of our physical bodies, but to know ourselves as entities, complete factors, capable of knowing all that goes on within and without. This spring of knowledge is tapped only by those who are willing to pay the price. The price is a complete surrender of ourselves, with a purification and a dedication that come only through prayer, meditation, and service. It is along the straight and narrow way, but it is open to all. The water of life is offered freely.

As entities, we are miniature copies of the universe, possessing physical, mental, and spiritual bodies. These bodies are so closely associated and related that the vibrations of one affect the other two. Our mental, especially, partakes of the other two: in the physical, as the conscious mind, and in the spiritual, as the superconscious mind.

Our bodies are temples of the living God. It has pleased God to so manifest Himself in the world. Our physical bodies are composite units of Creative Force manifesting in the material world. All parts of our bodies must work in unison, for should one war against another, discord would naturally follow. Each part has its functions, and it is so important that no other part can take its place; neither can any part be counted insignificant and useless.

Each organ has its individual functions and desires, which are in themselves holy. The senses make us conscious of the magnified desires or natures of our physical bodies. These are registered in the activities of our physical bodies in such a way that they are stamped upon our very faces. These senses are attuned to the physical, each vibrating according to the training and concentration of the physical forces, seeking expression of the inner self—of which our physical bodies are material representations. For not only do the impressions received through the senses show forth that which is magnified in a single appearance or experience, but also all impressions that have been received through all of our experiences, the registering being in our souls. These are registered in a material way in our physiognomy.

The Mental and Spiritual Bodies

In the same manner the desires of our mental and spiritual bodies build our individualities. This process of building has been going on for ages. The great factors of heredity, environment, karma, thought vibration, and the action of universal laws in the planes beyond the physical all have their influences, just as the desires and vibrations of the physical organs attract and build the composition of the physical body. We are the results not only of the development of the race before us but also of our individual development that has been going on since our creation as individual souls.

We are the sum total of all our experiences in every state of consciousness. "In my Father's house are many mansions"[1] (states of consciousness). In our body temples we are building, by thoughts and acts, not only our physical bodies, but the mental and spiritual bodies as well. Christ, the Master, said: "Not that which goeth into the mouth defileth a man; but that which cometh out of the mouth, this defileth a man."[2] Those of us who live to gratify only our fleshly bodies may be beautiful without, but we have so starved our souls that we are able to give out only that which makes for discord and corruption. In speaking of the scribes and Pharisees, Jesus said: "For ye are like unto whited sepulchres, which indeed appear beautiful outward, but are within full of dead men's bones, and of all uncleanness. Even so ye also outwardly appear righteous unto men, but within ye are full of hypocrisy and iniquity."[3] The same principle may be applied to right thinking, for we become what we think.

The soul will seek that which it has builded, not only in the material plane but in the universal, for "as a tree falls, so will it lie."[4] This is well understood if we know and study ourselves, for we will realize that each experience is a lesson to help bring the knowledge of the Whole, that "I and my Father are one."[5]

When we are seeking to lose ourselves in the Whole, it is possible to see ourselves as did the individual who had the following dream:

"I saw myself pass out of my body and become three bodies, physical, mental, and spiritual. At first the physical was the largest, but as the other two grew it gradually became smaller, until it finally faded into dust. The others then grew larger and moved around fourth-dimensionally."

When our acts and thoughts are measured by the standard of Christ, and when we reach the place where we desire only to be channels of blessings to others, we have lost sight of ourselves. Then we have the mind of Christ, for He came not to be ministered to, but to minister, and gave His life as a ransom for many.

Self in Relation to Others

We should let neither flattery, criticism, nor opinions of others turn us aside from those vital things for which we stand—those

[1]John 14:2   [2]Matt. 15:11   [3]Matt. 23:27, 28   [4]Eccles. 11:3   [5]John 10:30

things that are lifting us upward and building within us that which will endure until the end. Let us turn within to see if we are being true to ourselves when temptations arise. We know that we cannot be true to others unless we are first true to ourselves.

As we cultivate the ability to discriminate between right and wrong, good and evil, we are reaching the plane where we may be masters of our destiny. It is found in keeping the whole law: "Thou shalt love the Lord thy God with all thy heart . . . and thy neighbour as thyself."[6] This is a spiritual desire, for the carnal mind is envious. There is in all of us that still Voice that teaches sacrifice, love, and service, that warns of every catastrophe and protects from all danger. When it is listened to and followed, no mistakes are made, no wars are fought, no homes are broken up; for then we seek the good of our neighbors and the will of the Creator.

Let us dare to see ourselves as others see us. It is well to stand aside and see ourselves go by. Let us think back over the words and acts of the day, asking ourselves these questions: Why did we do this or that? Would we have acted before our God in the manner we acted before our neighbor? Are we expressing our concepts of God in our lives to those we contact? It is indeed true that "No man liveth to himself and no man dieth to himself."[7]

It is well to know what the other person thinks of us. We must, without any feeling of shame or humiliation, be willing to be measured by the standard that we have given one the impression we hold. It is our duty to study and discipline ourselves so that each word and each action may reflect just what we would be, and not let them be so different that they are not recognized as children of the same family.

While we are seeking to know ourselves through meditation or by taking an inventory, we are passing, as it were, signposts. We see a little light day by day, or catch a word here, an idea there, from those we contact, who help us to realize that all are traveling along the same road. Truly, the better we know ourselves, the better we understand others. Does it not make us more tolerant of our neighbors if we see them as we are, or as we have been?

Since service is the means of fulfilling our mission here, the

[6]Luke 10:27   [7]P.R. See Romans 14:7

question will naturally arise, "Who is this neighbor that we should serve?" It is that person who is in need of help, whether the individual be friend or foe, regardless of his or her race or creed. When Jesus defined this question, He said: "Behold my mother and my brethren! For whosoever shall do the will of my Father which is in heaven, the same is my brother, and sister, and mother."[8] If we measure our activities in the daily walks of life by the standard of the Christ, there will never be a regret. It is following the teachings of the Master that will lead more and more in the way toward a perfect understanding.

"Be what you seem. Live your creed. Hold up to earth the torch divine. Be what you pray to be made. Let the Master Jesus' steps be thine."[9]

Self in Relation to Creative Force

By keeping in touch with the Creative Force, we rise above the conditions where the blind lead the blind, and we know that we are guided by the All-Seeing Eye in all we are called to do.

> "If I ascend up into heaven, thou art there; if I make my bed in hell, behold, thou art there. If I take the wings of the morning, and dwell in the uttermost parts of the sea; even there shall thy hand lead me."   *Psalm 139:8-10*

Let us awake and know that God is speaking to us, leading us, and protecting us—that His Spirit is even now bearing witness with our spirit that we are children of God.

As the voices of our souls cry out to their Creator, let us not doubt the promise: "He that hungers and thirsts after righteousness shall be filled."[10] It may come as the wind, we may not know from whence, but all who seek will know that His name is "I am that I am"[11] who is speaking in His holy temple, the body. That is the true awakening. There is, indeed, a physical body, a mental body, and a spiritual body, and they are one—one in love, one in truth, one in service, and one in Him.

The Awakening of Self

Our physical bodies, our mental bodies, and our soul bodies are but shadows of the Triune. The body-physical is as human. The body-mental is as the savior of humanity, for it is through the application of the mental influences that we would control and

---

[8]Matt. 12:49-50   [9]P.E.   [10]P.R. See Matt. 5:6   [11]Exodus 3:14

build that which finds expression in the physical and in the soul. The body-soul is made in the image of the Creator, and made to be a companion in spirit. The physical body is the house, the home of the soul, during a sojourn in the material world. What we do with the opportunities that are presented in our various experiences gives expression to those powers that are lent to our souls and our bodies in their passage through the earth.

As the knowledge of the awakening of our soul forces is applied in our relationship to our fellow human beings, we come to realize our relationship to our Maker, for "As ye do it unto one of the least of these, ye do it unto Me."[12]

For us to be aware of our physical desires and appetites is physical awakening. To satisfy them selfishly is sin. This is illustrated in the experience of our first parents. "And when the woman saw that the tree was good for food, and that it was pleasant to the eyes, and a tree to be desired to make one wise, she took of the fruit thereof, and did eat, and gave also unto her husband with her; and he did eat."[13]

When we become aware that the mind can control the physical desires, then we have a mental awakening. "But Daniel purposed in his heart that he would not defile himself with . . . the king's meat, nor with the wine which he drank."[14] This is an illustration of one who stood firm in the light of a mental awakening, even though it was seemingly a sacrifice of life itself.

When we are conscious that we can reconcile the spirit within with the spirit without and know that they are one and are from the same source, God, then we have a spiritual awakening. This was manifested perfectly in Jesus, the Master, in His daily life among people.

An awakening is the natural thing, when we attune ourselves to the Source of all good, allowing His Spirit to bear witness with our spirit. We are awakened then to the knowledge that we are, indeed, children of God. We show forth our spiritual awakening by our patience, tolerance, long-suffering, and forbearance, not being willing that any should suffer, but that all should come to the knowledge of the Truth. When we practice these virtues in our daily lives we become masters among others.

[12]P.R. See Matt. 25:40   [13]Genesis 3:6   [14]Daniel 1:8

Conclusion

Let us realize that we should so live in body and in mind that we may be channels through which the Creative Forces may flow. Let us give more attention to our thoughts, for thoughts are deeds and are children of the union of the mind and the soul. What we think continually we become. What we cherish in our minds is built into our own physical bodies, becoming not only food for our souls, but also the soul's heritage in realms of other experiences.

Will is an attribute of the soul. We must recognize by exercising it that we either make ourselves one with our Maker, or separate ourselves from Him. With the will we can either adhere to or contradict those immutable laws set between the Creator and the created.

Let us determine within ourselves that a constructive program will be followed. The conditions of this program, then, require that a definite stand be taken by each of us. We are determined that we will adhere to it, no matter what we may suffer mentally or physically. We will trust in the divine Force within for the strength to endure and for the ability to say no when we should. We will consider the needs of others before our own.

May we study to show ourselves approved unto God in body, mind, and soul. May we become less and less aware of the desires to gratify the carnal forces of the body. Is our purpose in life to gain power, position, wealth, and to satisfy the longings of the flesh? Are we to lose our own souls by so doing? It is for us to choose. The Christ stands ready to help. Shall we bar the door of our own consciousness?

Father, as we seek to see and know Thy face, may we each, as individuals and as a group, come to know ourselves, even as we are known, that we—as lights in Thee—may give the better concept of Thy Spirit in this world.   *262-5*

Lesson III

WHAT IS MY IDEAL?

"Let this mind be in you, which was also in Christ Jesus."
Philippians 2:5

Affirmation

adistrust?

God, be merciful to me! Help Thou my unbelief! Let me see in Him that Thou would have me see in my fellow man. Let me see in my brother that I see in Him whom I worship.   _262-11_

III

WHAT IS MY IDEAL?

[Based on Edgar Cayce readings 262-11 through 262-14]

Introduction

What is an ideal? We are told that a mental concept or that conceived as a standard of perfection is an ideal. Mind is the builder. We are ever striving toward something to worship or something to love, be it physical, mental, or spiritual. From our experiences we form ideas; then through the action of imagination we sometimes confuse these ideas with ideals. An ideal is something beyond and above us toward which we build. To bind ourselves by calling our ideas ideals means the beginning of decay in the soul structure which we have builded. Our ideals are ever present; they are either consciously or unconsciously the bases for the motivating forces in our lives.

Ideals Grow with Development

In childhood the height which we hoped to reach was lower, by far, than the one that we placed as a goal in youth. We recall that the God we worshiped in our childhood has grown to the Spirit we now call "Abba, Father."[1] So, as we build onward and upward, our ideals enlarge until they reach the height of perfection, the Source of all Good, the Creative Energy of which we are manifestations.

From the physical, mental, and spiritual viewpoints our ideals are patterns by which we endeavor to shape our lives. We must understand the meaning of "The Oneness" and merge our physical and mental ideals with the spiritual ideal of the soul. Our spiritual pattern should not be trimmed to fit us, but we should grow to fit the pattern, whose Maker and Finisher is God.

[1]See Mark 14:36

His will not mine

The True Ideal

The true ideal is the highest spiritual attainment to be reached on this material plane; hence, it follows that our ideal must be found in Christ, who is the Way. One who climbs up some other way is a thief and a robber to oneself. All real seekers after truth recognize this, although they may have different ways of expressing it. The following quotations will illustrate this:

"To think, to speak, to act from the consciousness of my divine self that I may be like Him, that I may do the things He said I could do, and help those who have not heard His voice—this is my ideal."

"Thou glorious One, radiant beyond finite mind, I would manifest Thee more fully. Thou tender and loving Father, for Thy Son's sake give me the testimony of the Spirit to bear witness with my spirit that I am a child of God, and likewise help me fully to realize that my neighbor is one with Thee. Awaken me to the newness of life, peace, love, knowledge, and understanding—then I shall be reaching my true ideal."

"My ideal is spiritual in essence, regardless of where it leads. Christ the Guide, Christ the Leader, and Christ the Way. His ways are my ways, and His ambitions are my ambitions. To be Christlike is my ideal. We are the children of God and should act as such."

"My ideal is to be a perfect channel through which the will of the Father may be done, whether in the physical, the mental, or the spiritual plane, and to return to the Father from whence I came. My hopes and desires are in the One by whom all were created."

In Jesus we have the way, in Him we have the example, and in Him we have all the attributes of the Ideal manifested. His teachings and life of service to His fellow human beings show us the way we too must tread in attaining the height He reached. When in our relationship to our fellow human beings we are so perfected in the Christ Consciousness that each word, thought, and deed bring blessings to those we contact, then we may be sure that our ideal is the true one.

Attaining the Ideal

The ideal cannot be made by mortals, but must be of the

spiritual nature that has its foundation in Truth, in God. Know the first principle:

> The gift of God to man is an individual soul, which may be one with Him, and that may know itself to be one with Him and yet individual in itself, with the attributes of the Whole, yet not the Whole. *262-11*

Such must be the concept, or the ideal, whether of the imaginative, the mental, the physical, or the spiritual body. All may attain to such an ideal, yet never become the Ideal, but be one with the Ideal.

With this ideal once set, there will be no fear. There will come to each of us that grace to dare to be a Daniel, to dare to stand alone. We attain our ideal by seeing the Father in others. Let our prayer be,

> God, be merciful to me! Help Thou my unbelief! Let me see in Him that Thou would have me see in my fellow man. Let me see in my brother that I see in Him whom I worship. *262-11*

We reach this vision through Christ. It takes the penetrating light of His Spirit to discern the divine spark in fallen humanity. It takes the mind of Christ to bless and not condemn, to love and not censure. The fields are now ripe unto harvest, but the laborers are few. We must work, work, for the night of unbelief and doubt comes.

It is our heritage to catch the true concept of the Divine in all and to be, in truth, co-workers with God. As there is raised in ourselves more and more of the Christ Consciousness, we become free indeed, and with freedom comes the awakening—the awakening to the realization of the Ideal.

As we see others as the Christ sees them and strive to consecrate ourselves to Him, then our daily acts, our words, and our thoughts will bring that understanding and realization of the Ideal manifested in us as well as in others. Let us look for good in everyone, speaking neither evil, harsh, nor unkind words to any at any time.

Let us do all that we know to do, in love, and leave the results with God. Let us hold fast to that which we have purposed in our inner selves, knowing that no emergency in a material way or manner may arise that cannot find its solution in spiritual inspiration, for His promises are sure. Offenses may arise, yet with each and every fear there is that from within which will quiet our troubled minds, even as He quelled the tempest on the sea. As we seek, we find; as we knock, we are heard. If we are timid, fearful, or overcautious in giving out the hope which has sustained us, then we grow more weak and fearful ourselves.

Conclusion

Have we chosen the spiritual Ideal? Are the things in our own lives measured by that Ideal? When we sincerely examine ourselves and know that our standard is what we see in the other individual and come to realize that our God is manifesting in and through that person, we know that the Ideal we are setting for ourselves is one that will lift us up and cause us to be merciful, even as our heavenly Father is merciful. Then we may be assured of the peace that passes understanding.

What is our Ideal? The Christ-Way. Let us not be anxious, but wait on the Lord, knowing that He is faithful who promised, "If any man hear my voice, and open the door, I will come in to him, and will sup with him, and he with me."[2]

[2]Rev. 3:20

Lesson IV

FAITH

"Above all, taking the shield of faith, wherewith ye shall be able to quench all the fiery darts of the wicked."   Ephesians 6:16

Affirmation

Create in me a pure heart, O God. Open Thou my heart to the faith Thou hast implanted in all that seek Thy face. Help Thou mine unbelief in my God, in my neighbor, in myself.   *262-13*

IV

FAITH

[Based on Edgar Cayce readings 262-13 through 262-17]

What Is Faith?

Faith is an attribute of the soul. It is the inner spiritual knowledge of the Creative Forces of the universe. As we become cognizant of the physical body through the senses, so we may become aware of the soul through the activity of its attributes. Faith may be denied or renounced until it ceases to exist within the consciousness of the physical mind. It can be acknowledged and exercised until it will remove mountains. That which is brought into consciousness through the activity of spiritual forces, manifesting in and through the spiritual force of the individual, becomes the essence of faith itself. Hence, it has been termed by many that faith, pure faith, accepts or rejects without basis of reason, beyond the ken and scope of that which is perceived through—that which we bring to our activity through— the five senses.

"Faith," as defined by Barnabas, "is the substance of things hoped for, the evidence of things not seen."[1] Faith knows that it has already received and acts accordingly, doubting nothing. It is the builder of the seemingly impossible. It is that which has brought into manifestation all that has ever existed. God is, faith is. It is the evidence of God's promise fulfilled. Man's divine privilege is to accept, use, develop, and enjoy the fruits of faith.

In the material world we often mistake confidence for faith. We are prone to depend upon our physical senses, forgetting that they are deceptive. This is not faith, but confidence—for confidence comes through the physical senses. When trials and disasters

[1]P.R. See Hebrew 11:1

43

arise, that are seemingly beyond our power to control, we begin to sink, and immediately in hopelessness and distress we cry out, "Lord, help me, I perish!" It is then that the Voice speaks, "O ye of little faith!"[2]

Let us examine ourselves and see whether we are holding to faith or confidence. We must view spiritual things from spiritual standpoints and accept them in a spiritual way.

Many say, "We have faith," but they begin to explain that it applies to mental and not to material things. We say, "We believe, but—" which means there is doubt, the very opposite of faith. Remember, when we entered this material plane, we became subject to material laws. It is the failure of our senses to perceive and fully to understand these laws that brings many of us to the point where we have little real faith.

There is a world before us to be understood: the mysteries of the universe, the law of love, the power of thought, and the matchless gift of faith. We stumble, we falter, even when we have the divine promise, "If ye have faith as a grain of mustard seed, ye shall say unto this mountain, Remove hence to yonder place; and it shall remove; and nothing shall be impossible unto you."[3] With such a promise, should we not cry out, "Lord, I believe; help Thou mine unbelief"?[4]

Need of Faith

Faith is victory, for where there is faith rightly placed, there is no failure, but true success. "Be thou faithful unto death, and I will give thee a crown of life";[5] that is, be full of faith and have as a reward life's crowning glories. We know that all our development, physical, mental, and spiritual, depends upon our faith in God, in our fellow human beings, and in ourselves. Just in proportion to the amount of faith we place in God and in ourselves, just so great is our development. Why not take God at His word, letting our faith become a living faith by acting in the manner that shows to the world that we know ourselves to be children of God. There is no other way to real victory.

Let us have more faith in our fellow human beings. We may not agree with them, but who knows whether they are not more in line with the divine plan than if they were following our lead? It is well to remember that our Ideal is manifested through our

[2]Luke 12:28   [3]Matt. 17:20   [4]Mark 9:24   [5]Rev. 2:10

fellow humans as well as through ourselves, and it is, therefore, more necessary for us to trust them, even though appearances may be against it.

It is not only our privilege, but our duty to have faith in ourselves. We are workers together with God, and when we doubt ourselves, we doubt the God within us. He has promised, "I will never leave thee, nor forsake thee."[6] Call to mind the words: "I can do all things through Christ which strengtheneth me."[7] In His Name we are more than conquerors. It is only by having the faith of a little child in the abiding presence of the Christ that we can hope to inherit the kingdom.

Faith is a bridge that spans the gulf from the seen to the unseen. It is often all we have left when everything seems against us. With this in mind, how diligently should we cultivate and seek to increase our faith when all is going well with us, in order that it may be a strong fortress when the storms of life begin to beat upon us. Lord, increase our faith!

How Faith Is Developed

Faith is developed by the use of it. It cannot be taught or forced, neither can true faith be destroyed. Through the exercising of faith, we are able to give enlightenment to others.

Let the mind be in us that was in Jesus the Christ; then there will come faith that is sufficient unto every need, even that faith which removes mountains, changes the destiny of nations, yea, and even brings worlds into existence. Do we believe this? Then, how may this be accomplished? By opening our hearts in meditation to the unseen forces that surround the throne of grace, beauty, and might, and at the same time by throwing about us the protection found in the thought of the Christ, we can accomplish this. (See 262-3.) Then let us add to our faith works which show forth attributes that are expressions of His Spirit in the world. Thus shall our faith develop and become to us evidence of things not seen. We must show by our actions in our daily lives that we believe, that we have faith, and that we know as we use what we have, more will be given.

In times of trial, let us think of the faith that has sustained others in troubles far greater than ours. When our conscious minds would magnify our doubts, let us awaken our faith by

[6]Hebrews 13:5   [7]Phil. 4:13

rising above the cries of the flesh. Are we not children of the Most High? Let us hold steadfastly to this gift that is God-given, that will lead us upward along the way of life.

In studying and applying cooperation, in using the knowledge we have gained in knowing ourselves, in holding to our ideal, and in never letting our faith falter, we are building step by step that which may become living truth in the lives of individuals with whom we come in contact. As we apply what we know, there is given a greater understanding of how our faith may increase and become a living thing in our experience. We are in our daily lives reflections of what we worship. Let our light so shine that others seeing the light in us may glorify God.

Where Faith Abounds

Only into the heart that is free from selfish love can there come a faith that will sustain in all conditions of life. Our faith must be a sustaining faith, a living faith, one that we can try out daily and know to be sure and steadfast. Where there is real faith, there is no fear, for with faith in the abiding love of the Father, what cause is there for us to have an anxious moment?

Every step of the way is shown to us who are faithful, for His word is a lamp to our feet. When the way is dark and barriers seem impassable, then the light of the Sun of righteousness[8] shines forth to us who abide in the promises He made.

When faith abides within, we have true freedom and the assurance that we have no master save Jesus the Christ, and that we are protected by the strong arm of the Father. The feeling of security, protection, and peace that passes understanding is found nowhere else. Faith is the promise sent on before to show that whatever we ask we have.

Self-Analysis Necessary

The solution of mental problems is more important to us than physical, although this does not seem true to the average individual lost in the twisted paths of materialism. Free the mind and the battle is almost won. Mental anguish is far greater than physical, for the mind can conquer physical pain, but it is necessary for the spiritual forces to aid the suffering mind.

The savages worship a god who will send rain and sunshine

[8]See Mal. 4:2

and protect them from lightning. The philosopher seeks a god who will give peace in mind and soul. Do we know in whom we believe? If so, then the ideal or standard toward which we move becomes the basis for the activity of faith in constant action from the mental, imaginative, and spiritual forces. Thus we may express or bring into manifestation that which is held as our ideal— not for self-exaltation, but rather to show the blessings we have received and to see them manifested in the lives of others.

Let us look within ourselves and know that we are workers together with God. We should analyze ourselves to find out just where the flesh is weak, where we are most likely to fail, and then seek a constant reinforcement of spirit that will make us hold on with unwavering faith to our Ideal.

Evidences of Faith

"When the day is dark and the way is obscure and we can still hold on, there is evidence that there is faith. When the sea of life is rough and we have the courage to step out boldly on the troubled waters, it is because there is still the divine gift at the very center of our being that is saying, 'Peace, be still,'[9] for 'I am with thee and will not leave thee.'[10] We have heard it. We can hear it always, if we will only take the time to listen."

"When doubts arise and the clouds of despair are thick, do we not call out in the night, 'My God, my God, why hast thou forsaken me?'[11] Does not an answer come? Are we not stronger by having an experience that gives us a better understanding of our neighbor who suffers in the same manner?"

"Some years ago, I was with a party that was visiting a noted cavern. Everyone seemed very happy. After being in the cavern for a short time, I became very much frightened. The thought came to me, 'How terrible, how dreadful it would be, if we could not find our way out!' The very air seemed to press in upon me. Ages seemed to pass. Then came the Voice that has sustained me so often: 'Lo, I am with you always.'[12] 'Be not afraid.'[13] With these words there came the strengthening of my faith."

"When loved ones are lingering in pain and no earthly help is nigh, are there not evidences of the faith of our fathers revived, when we pray and receive help? It brings the greatest comfort to us, not only in the trying times but at all times, to know inwardly

[9]Mark 4:39 [10]P.R. [11]Mark 15:34 [12]See Matt. 28:20 [13]John 6:20

that His promises are sure."

Reward of Faith

Our rewards are in proportion to the faith we exercise.
"According to your faith be it with you."[14] "Whatsoever ye shall
ask in prayer, believing, ye shall receive."[15] There is no limit to
the reward. It is ours to measure, and ours to claim. "Prove me
... if I will not open you the windows of heaven and pour you out
a blessing, that there shall not be room enough to receive it."[16]

Let us open ourselves as channels, and have complete faith in
God, for the battle is the Lord's. It remains to be seen what we can
do when we give ourselves unreservedly into the hands of the
Father. "And I will pray the Father and He shall give you another
comforter, even the Spirit of Truth, who will guide you into all
Truth."[17]

"And what shall I more say? for the time would fail me to tell
of Gedeon, and of Barak, and of Samson, and of Jephthae; of
David also, and Samuel, and of the prophets: Who through faith
subdued kingdoms, wrought righteousness, obtained promises
... And these all, having obtained a good report through faith,
received not the promise: God having provided some better thing
for us, that they without us should not be made perfect. Wherefore
seeing we also are compassed about with so great a cloud of
witnesses, let us lay aside every weight, and the sin which doth
so easily beset us, and let us run with patience the race that is set
before us, Looking unto Jesus the author and finisher of our
faith."[18]

---

[14]Matt. 9:29   [15]Matt. 21:22   [16]Mal. 3:10   [17]P.R. See John 14:16; 16:13
[18]Hebrews 11:32-33, 39-40; 12:1, 2

Lesson V

VIRTUE AND UNDERSTANDING

"Finally, brethren, whatsoever things are true, whatsoever things are honest, whatsoever things are just, whatsoever things are pure, whatsoever things are lovely, whatsoever things are of good report; if there be any virtue, and if there be any praise, think on these things."   Philippians 4:8

Affirmation

Let virtue and understanding be in me, for my defense is in Thee, O Lord, my Redeemer; for Thou hearest the prayer of the upright in heart. *262-17*

V

VIRTUE AND UNDERSTANDING

[Based on Edgar Cayce readings 262-18 through 262-20]

Introduction

In defining virtue and understanding, we must remember that these words are used here in their fuller meaning as expressions or activities of the soul or spirit forces, not as mental or emotional concepts. To establish a common ground, let us say that to be true to that which is pure in our purposes is virtue. Virtue is full cooperation that prepares the way for enlightening and uplifting humanity. Virtue is keeping ourselves in tune with Creative Force, enabling us to know ourselves as we are known by others. Virtue is holding steadfastly to the Ideal that is set in Him, the Lord of Lords and King of Kings. Virtue is pureness of heart, pureness of soul, and pureness of mind that come through His Spirit bearing witness with our spirit. Virtue is the seasoning of faith, the essence of hope, and the crowning element of truth—an attribute of God.

True understanding is beyond the reason of the senses. It is the power to experience and interpret the laws that govern the expression of Creative Force, or God, in and through the physical, mental, and spiritual bodies of humanity. Where there is virtue there will be understanding, for one follows the other. Understanding is the reward of virtue. With virtue, therefore, comes understanding, for the two are as the tenon and the mortise; they fit one with the other. Knowledge is not always understanding. Daily, many experience miracles of which they have no understanding. Few that have mere knowledge get understanding. An understanding of the mysteries of life comes to those only who make a close approach to the Throne. We may

51

know the course of the stars, the intricate formulae of
mathematics, and the secrets of sciences, but we cannot
understand God's laws until we have experienced that closeness
with the Divine that makes us realize that we are part of His
laws, rather than mere observers of them. It was no miracle to
those who understood Stephen when he said, "Behold, I see the
heavens opened, and the Son of Man standing on the right hand
of God."[1] It was no miracle to the Master when He fed the five
thousand with five loaves and two fishes, for He understood the
law of supply. It requires an understanding of God's law (love),
when such a message is heard even today as, "Lo, I am present
with you in this room—I have chosen you as ye have chosen me.
Keep the way thou knowest, keep the path thou hast trod, for He
is able to deliver thee in every trial, and unto that one who is
faithful comes the crown of life. As I am lifted up in thy
consciousness, so will I be lifted up in the consciousness of
others."[2] With such an understanding comes a finer and more
sincere relationship with others, and a higher spiritual concept
of self. We link virtue and understanding because they are
expressions of the activities of the soul forces. Virtue built into
the mind is the only sure path to true understanding. Knowledge
assists when it is in harmony and in accord with the Ideal;
otherwise, it may become a barrier, a curse, and a dark pit from
which it is hard to escape.

Virtue and Understanding Are Spiritual

Those of us who seek virtue and understanding must walk
with God. We never sink so low that we do not at some time feel
a longing to look up, and to seek something higher than our own
selfish desires. Often it takes only a song, a kind word, or a
friendly deed to cause the fire of hope to leap and such a prayer
to be uttered as "Lord, be merciful to me a sinner!"

We may be counted worthy to point out the way only after we
have walked the way with Him, who was tempted in all ways like
unto us, yet without sin.

If our hearts are open to the consciousness that comes from
abiding in Him, there will be no misunderstandings, for the
power of the Holy Spirit will awaken in each of us that which was
ours in the beginning. The desire for virtue and understanding

[1]Acts 7:56   [2]P.R.

is already within. Spirit cries to spirit, "Purify me, cleanse me! Give me back my first estate, my virtue, my understanding, my God!" "As the hart panteth after the water brooks, so panteth my soul after Thee, O God."[3]

May our aspirations be expressed in the following words:

O Thou divine and celestial spark, alive in some, dormant in others—Virtue, Understanding, Creative Force, God—have Thy own way in our hearts and lives, we pray!

Virtue and Understanding Are Essential to Right Living

Both virtue and understanding are essential to right living, or righteous living. They are needed in meeting the daily problems of life that arise within us as well as in our relationships with others. We sincerely desire that our standards be correct, but none of us can choose aright unless we are guided by the Holy Spirit. It is hard to know the original cause or the final result of a decision influencing another. We may not know what trial or tribulation may have caused a neighbor to err. If we know, it is because we have ourselves experienced some similar tribulation. It is then that our standards are measured by Him who abides within our holy temple, and they fit perfectly with the Ideal within our less fortunate neighbor. We have no cause to find fault or condemn.

Virtue and understanding are the requisites for spiritual work. What we do not possess we cannot give. What we do not live we cannot teach others to live. Unless we are pure, how can we expect others to be pure? Our very words and acts condemn us. We must be and know before we can direct, or before we can rightly guide others who are seeking the safe harbor.

There is a desire in each of us to live better day by day. We wish to reach a certain goal. If we are choosing the highest, the best, we will not be satisfied with anything less. It is well for us to remember that the highest goal is not reached at a single bound, but step by step—here a little, there a little. It is encouraging to know that no good deed is lost, not even a good intention; but all are built within our very souls and will bear fruits, some thirty, some fifty and some a hundredfold. It is by deeds, righteous deeds, that we rise. "We climb to heaven leaning on the arm of a

[3]Psalm 42:1

brother whom we have helped." (See 281-4.)

The Way to Virtue and Understanding

The way to virtue and understanding is through prayer and meditation. The approach to all understanding must come from a proper concept of our needs in the physical, the mental, and the spiritual phases of our lives. This is the approach of the Master Jesus.

Others may point the way, but have they the virtue and understanding of Him who said, "I am the way, the truth, and the life"?[4] He proclaimed no way except the one He, Himself, had trod. He so lived the way that He could say, "Follow me."[5] The way is open to all.

We are moving along the path when we begin to see ourselves as others see us, when no unkind thought of our neighbor is allowed to lodge in our hearts, and when we seek earnestly to be pure in heart, pure in mind, pure in body, and pure in soul.

The way is straight and narrow, so narrow that we must have no will but the Father's, that we must have no purpose but to do His work, and that we must have no aim but to reach the Christ Consciousness. This leads to virtue and understanding. "Seek, and ye shall find; knock, and it shall be opened unto you."[6]

Personal Experiences

"I have found the way. It is through divine love, and it is for all who desire it. I prayed seven years for divine love. It is a living thing within me, giving me strength to love those who have wronged me, giving me the sight to see good in those who would do evil. It is in me the healing power. I give thanks that I now recognize the God within me who is helping me to express divine qualities."

If we would have virtue, then let us step out on faith—faith in the purity of self, faith in the perfection of our neighbor, and faith in the promises of God. Virtue is the reward of faith, and understanding is the reward of virtue. Through faith the veil is lifted and we can go within ourselves, within the holy of holies and be transformed into the image and likeness of the Son of God.

"I did not feel I had the necessary virtue for an upright life. After much thought and meditation, the words came to me,

[4]John 14:6   [5]P.R. See John 21:22   [6]Luke 11:9

'Faith is the chief cornerstone.' This helped me, for I knew that I could exercise faith. I then began to give thanks that I, through faith in the Christ, had virtue, a cleansing of body, soul, and spirit. Understanding came to me."

We must have implicit faith in God and in His promises, if we would have the cleansing power of His Spirit manifesting in our lives. We must have full faith in our neighbor, if we hope to be as pure as we demand him or her to be. We must have more faith in ourselves and in the power of the Spirit ever ready to manifest in and through us, if we expect to do our greatest work. Unless we have faith, how can we expect to see the glories of God? One that doubts is condemned. It is only through faith that we are justified, for belief in God is counted unto us for righteousness.

Virtue Is a Defense, Understanding Is a Weapon

Virtue has the dynamic power of the Holy Spirit. It strengthens the spiritual quality of humankind and engenders a greater knowledge of the Maker and a greater faith in Him. The more we open our hearts as a channel of blessings to others, the more power we possess. Keeping the channel clear, open, and ready to be used, we see the seemingly impossible begin to take place and we come to realize that no weapon that is formed against us shall prosper. Happy are we when protected by the impregnable defense found in the same pureness of ourselves that we demand of others.

Virtue is a defense against all temptation to censure, condemn, or criticize—for with it we see with eyes that are looking for the pure. We see behind the vice of other souls, made in the image of their Maker. We feel that they need our love and our help along the way. With virtue within, we never retard the development of others.

As with virtue comes understanding, so with understanding comes divine light. Understanding is a strong and tried weapon whose blade is never bent. It has ever been a weapon in the endless warfare for truth. When once the enemy is conquered, it is at the same time won as an ally, for it stands in awe in the presence of a power that gives an understanding of its real intents and purposes. Only with virtue and understanding can we rise above the tumult in the battle of life, and, with the

Master, pass through the midst of it and go our way. How simple when we understand! How wonderful when we are pure in heart, pure in mind, and pure in spirit!

The Effects of Virtue and Understanding on Ourselves and Others

Virtue and understanding have to do primarily with ourselves and with our relationship to the Creative Forces. They are reflected in our judgment of others, for our conduct is a reflection of our inner thoughts. To think nobly is to act nobly. It is a privilege to think, provided we think with a mind that is in tune with the ideal that is set in the Christ. We may compare the daily building of ourselves, mentally, physically, and spiritually, to the construction of a house. Are we choosing those attributes that will help our development? Are we casting aside the imperfect stones, using only the good? Are we placing them evenly in line? Are we ready to be passed on by the divine Inspector? If we can answer these questions in the affirmative, then we are hastening our development toward God. The quality of the structure depends upon us and upon us only. We are building for ourselves either hovels or holy temples.

No one liveth to oneself. How we live, act, and think not only is reflected in ourselves but also has its effect upon others. As we put into practice love, mercy, justice, patience, and forgiveness, others catch the same spirit. This is illustrated by one who came in contact with those who had received spiritual cleansing. "They made me better," she said, "gave me back my living faith, instilled in me a desire to realize—that God lives and is speaking through all people. They gave me hope and new interest in life. Before I met them my worship was form; afterwards it became more spiritual and I began to reach out for the joy that seemed to be theirs."

Finally, we know we have passed from death unto life because we love. We know that new life now courses through us, and that a new and strange peace is ours that makes us in accord with divine will. What we once despised now we cherish, and the world we formerly cherished now ceases to attract. We give thanks to God for this unspeakable gift of spiritual understanding which is now ours through the cleansing power of the Holy Spirit.

May the following words be ever upon our lips:

Let virtue and understanding be in me, for my defense is in Thee, O Lord, my Redeemer; for Thou hearest the prayer of the upright in heart.   *262-17*

Lesson VI

FELLOWSHIP

"If we walk in the light, as He is in the light, we have fellowship one with another."   I John 1:7

Affirmation

How excellent is Thy name in the earth, O Lord! Would I have fellowship with Thee, I must show brotherly love to my fellow man. Though I come in humbleness and have aught against my brother, my prayer, my meditation, does not rise to Thee. Help Thou my efforts in my approach to Thee.   *262-21*

VI

FELLOWSHIP

[Based on Edgar Cayce readings 262-21 through 262-23]

Introduction

In preparation for the task before us, let us become more conscious of the divine Spirit within, that we may go on. May we face the issues before us as those called for a purpose. May we rely on His promises, for while we are often weak and selfish—and the work is great—He will encourage our spirits, our hearts, with the presence of His Holy Spirit, so that there may be no idleness or delay in us.

A spark of the Divine that is forever seeking its source is within each of us. As we develop our spiritual forces, our soul forces within, we fan this spark into a flame which brings realization of our oneness and fellowship with the Creator of all things. There is a longing in our hearts for this fellowship—an urge driving us hither and thither in search of happiness and satisfaction, onward in search of God.

In the beginning, all knew a perfect fellowship with the Father, and in the knowledge and understanding of this fellowship all walked and talked with God. Again, this same fellowship is offered to all, a promise of the Father, through the Son. It is the reflection of this fellowship which expresses itself in our love for our fellow human beings, whom we innately feel to be one with us as part of the all-inclusive Whole. As we manifest love toward our neighbor, we increase or awaken our consciousness to a more complete fellowship with the Father, and we more fully realize that He moves within others as He moves within us. The family of humankind is but a shadow of fellowship with the Father. It is a true expression of the fellowship that exists in spirit.

Am I My Brother's Keeper?

Thousands of years ago there arose a question in humanity's heart, "Am I my brother's keeper?"[1] It is still being asked. Until this is fully answered in our hearts in God's way and put into practice in our lives, we cannot hope to have the fellowship that is our rightful heritage. When we fail to reach "the mark of the high calling" that is realized in service, we endeavor to justify ourselves by making the old inquiry, only to receive the answer, "The voice of thy brother's blood crieth unto me from the ground."[2] No wonder we are miserable and cast down, and have fears that paralyze our efforts. Is it not because we know in our hearts that sin lies at our door?

"Behold, what manner of love the Father hath bestowed upon us, that we should be called the sons of God."[3] God gives only love to His children and pities them even as earthly parents pity their children. It is only when we sever relationship from divine Love by failing to suffer with our fellow humans, to bear their burdens, and to forgive them that we are out of harmony and sympathy with all that makes life worth living—fellowship with the Father. Have we not at some time realized this?

If we would be in a position to commune with the Spirit within and if we would seek to know His face, then let us be kind and gentle, compassionate and loving to others less fortunate. Manifesting love for our neighbor is manifesting love for God, in whom "we live and move and have our being."[4]

We are enjoined not merely to ignore the shortcomings of our neighbors, but to love them in spite of their shortcomings and to show such faith in the power of the Spirit within them that they will catch our vision and in time come to realize their strength and seek to rise to higher planes of consciousness. We need not flatter them or lead them to overestimate their strength; rather we should help them to understand themselves and to know that they have a friend who will stand by in time of need—one who will extend a hand if they are about to fall into temptation. This answers the whole duty of humanity to humanity, of neighbor to neighbor, and of the individual to his or her Maker, for "Inasmuch as ye have done it unto one of the least of these my brethren, ye have done it unto me."[5]

The test is this: Are we willing to deal with others as we wish

---

[1]Genesis 4:9   [2]Genesis 4:10   [3]I John 3:1   [4]P.R. See Acts 17:28   [5]Matt. 25:40

them to deal with us? May we ever be bound together in service
to others through the fellowship which we have in Him.

Our Fellowship with God

If we wish to know how we stand with God, let us examine
ourselves and see how we feel toward our neighbor. This
companionship that we are seeking with God is found in the
friendliness we show our neighbor. It is evident that our actions,
our words, and our thoughts indicate too plainly our failure to
seek fellowship with the Father. Let us examine ourselves that
we may know what is buried in our hearts and minds that may
be blinding us or binding us; and if we have anything against
another, let us pray for forgiveness, knowing that His mercy is
sufficient for all.

Seek God where He may be found, even in the heart of a
neighbor. How well do we know God? Just as well as we seek to
know and understand our fellow human beings, and just as well
as we seek to magnify the divine consciousness in them. Do we
seek far for the Divine in this direction? Do we not judge our
neighbors from appearances rather than by righteous judgment?
Do we not often overlook the motive which may have prompted
their misconduct? Do we realize that deep down in the heart of
our neighbors there lies buried a celestial fire that burns ever
before the altar of our God? Then let us seek them out and, in
spite of the rebuffs that we may receive, love them, not for what
they appear to be, but for what they really are—not because they
are human and need our sympathy, but because within them
there is the Divine that merits our adoration.

What is more beautiful than fellowship! The Master sought it,
that He might do the works of God. He did not withdraw from
people, but mingled with them, sharing their sorrows, living
their lives, and relieving their sufferings. We cannot hope to
emulate His example, however, unless we abide in the Spirit that
gives the strength. "I am the vine, ye are the branches. He that
abideth in me, and I in him, the same bringeth forth much fruit;
for without me ye can do nothing."[6] The Master taught that love
and service go hand in hand. What greater love could He have
shown than to lay down His life in service for His fellow human
beings; yet that is just how far the Master went to demonstrate

[6]John 15:5

His power over sin, death, and the grave, that those who seek life might know the way. May the Spirit help us to be willing to serve, and to see in our neighbor his or her higher self at all times, in all places, and under all circumstances.

If we would have fellowship, we must rely on His promises and keep His commandments, which are not grievous. The greatest commandment "that ye love one another," He called a new commandment, and it is still new to many of His followers.

We affirm that we want to know God, but do we really mean it? If we are really sincere, will we not be eager to sacrifice our desires, our opinions, and our whims, that the wonders found in the knowledge and understanding of the works of the Creator, our God and Father, may be revealed to us? May we not be willing to endure, that we may be counted worthy to share in the glory to be revealed to those who have given themselves wholly to His service? How easy the way when self is lost in Him! How easy to follow when we have been told to use what we have and more will be given.

Let us remember the Master's words to Simon: "Feed my sheep."[7] None of us can approach the Father with any degree of assurance when we feel and know in our hearts that we are out of harmony with ourselves or others. We are out of harmony with ourselves when we lack faith in ourselves, or when we minimize the power of the God within and forget that all power in heaven and earth is committed to our keeping—if we will attune ourselves to the Infinite Source of that power. We are out of harmony with others when we think of them as less divine than ourselves or as possessing less divine power, love, and mercy. Therefore, it is necessary to begin with ourselves to purge our hearts and minds and to become more conscious of the divine Spirit within others. This is necessary if we hope to have the fellowship with the Father that will cause us to realize our oneness with Him.

Prayer and meditation are the essential factors that will keep alive within us this perfect harmony. Are we seeking this fellowship? Would we have God draw nigh unto us? If so, then let us draw nigh unto God, approaching often the Throne of Grace, with mercy in our hearts.

"The heart is deceitful above all things, and desperately wicked,"[8] that is, the unregenerated heart, the heart that knows

[7]P.R. See John 21:16   [8]Jer. 17:9

not the cleansing of the Spirit or the awakening of the presence of God. Let us search our hearts. "If our heart condemn us, God is greater than our heart, and knoweth all things."[9] He knows our joys and sorrows; He knows how we have tried and, therefore, in spite of our failures, shows love and mercy. If our hearts condemn us not, then we have faith in God, faith that He will keep His promises.

Let us be ever ready to forgive. This is the way that God deals with us. He has pardoned our sins and blotted out our transgressions. How much more should we be willing to forgive others! If the thoughts, deeds, or acts of others have caused us pain, let them not be magnified in our own mind or charged to their account. Let us who have pledged our loyalty bear the cross, since we have the promise of the crown. Let us help our fellow human beings by our patience and forbearance and show them that love is a living thing. What great love hath the Father bestowed upon us that we might show forth His glory among all people!

Let us strive to be kind, training ourselves to be considerate of those who do not seem to appreciate it. Yes, be kind when it is the hardest. It is worth the trial, not for the reward we may expect from others, but because we cannot allow anything to mar the fellowship we would have with the Father. One unkind word may not leave a lifelong pang in the heart of another, but it will place us so out of harmony with all that we count worthwhile that its effects will follow us perhaps through many years. Great kindness may be shown through little deeds. One who gives a word of comfort to the disheartened will have one's reward. Though this is a small service, it may help as nothing else would help. Let us not count any good act lost. No seed falls to the ground without the Father's knowledge. It was only a cup of water to the tired Master at the well that set the occasion which brought many out of the city seeking to know more about the water of life. May we lose no opportunity to bind up the brokenhearted, to pour oil on the troubled waters, or to heed the command, "Comfort ye, comfort ye my people, saith your God."[10]

Let us remember that we shall give account for every idle thought; therefore, let us think on those things that make for love for others. As we develop step by step, here a little, there a little, we learn cooperation, we get better acquainted with ourselves,

[9]I John 3:20   [10]Isaiah 40:1

trust more fully in our Ideal, have our faith strengthened, gain virtue and understanding, and more and more become aware of our fellowship with the Father and our duty to others.

Fellowship with God, the Need of the World

The crying need among people of all ages has been that individuals must understand themselves, their relationship to their neighbor and to their Maker, and know that they are inseparable. These are one. It is impossible to separate God from His creations, for He manifests through them.

It is impossible to love God and hate our neighbors, whose souls are made in the image and likeness of God. Love and hate cannot live in the same heart. Too many of us count fellowship unimportant. Many of us are selfish and are neglecting to let those attributes that reflect fellowship have a place in our lives. If we are making this mistake, we know it, our neighbor knows it, and more than all, the Father knows it. The world is poorer because of the stumbling blocks we have put in the way of others. In this we are not only blocking our own development but also the very purposes for which we were created.

This fellowship with God, of which the world is so much in need, does not simply embrace kindness and gentleness toward friends but also includes love for enemies. This relationship to God will likewise make us see that to love our enemies does not mean simply to have the right attitude toward them, but rather to have in our hearts a yearning for them to know the Way. In their most terrible acts we can see a power for good misdirected. This attitude will help the world to better understand the obstacles and trials of others, including other nations, since peace on earth and good will toward all must first be experienced by the individual before it may be realized among nations.

With this knowledge of the need of fellowship, how can we hold a spirit of revenge, dislike, or judgment? Would we dare to bind others by our thoughts?

Love and brotherhood, reflections of fellowship with the Father, instilled into the hearts and lives of all, would bring this world into such a happy state that the millennium would be here in deed and in truth. It will be well for us to examine ourselves in order to know whether we as individuals are doing our full part.

Are we fulfilling the law of love toward rich and poor, high and low, saint and sinner, friend and foe?

There is no better place to practice love for others than in the home. Just watch its effects upon members of the family. If at home we cannot answer kindly, it will be better not to answer at all. It is far better for an angry thought to die unexpressed than for it to kill the good in the life of the speaker and retard the development of the one to whom it is addressed.

Duty of Those Who Have Fellowship with the Father

"Ye have not chosen me, but I have chosen you."[11] In fellowship there comes a duty to others. There are certain bonds to be kept, and certain laws to be understood and reverenced. "Who shall stand in his holy place? He that hath clean hands, and a pure heart"[12]—such have fellowship with the Father. They delight in His laws and understand and cherish them.

Yet many of us may complain that the way is hard and that the obligations are many and heavy to bear. Are we not judged out of our own mouths? Should we not rather take Him at His word and know the truth of His assurance, "My yoke is easy, and my burden is light,"[13] and that He will place no burden upon us that we are not able to bear?

One who sought true fellowship told of the experience in these words: "I saw a vision. In it I was able to discover what it meant to be selfish. I beheld myself in the school of life, using what little spiritual food I had for my own benefit. I was sitting on the side of a hill, eating. I soon realized that the ground upon which I was sitting was beginning to crumble. My food was also rapidly diminishing. A voice said, 'To him that hath not, it shall be taken away from him even that he seemeth to have.'[14] Suddenly, I became aware of my destitute position. My food was gone, the earth was receding, and great billows of water were about to overtake me. I arose and began to climb upward, slowly, laboriously. I eagerly sought and accepted help from those I had formerly considered on lower spiritual planes than I. These words came to me: 'Whatsoever a man soweth, that shall he also reap,'[15] and, 'All things whatsoever ye would that men should do to you, do ye even so to them.' "[16]

[11]John 15:16 [12]Psalm 24:3, 4 [13]Matt. 11:30 [14]P.R. See Luke 8:18 [15]Gal. 6:7 [16]Matt. 7:12

That which we think, we become. That which we are, we reflect. That which we reflect, others judge us to be. We may be mistaken in our estimation of ourselves and others may misjudge us, but God looks on the heart and knows all things. He knows our purposes and what we are capable of becoming. The Master said, "Thou art Peter, and upon this rock I will build my church,"[17] though He knew that Peter in his weakness would deny Him. It is our duty to walk before others in such a manner that they may see the good within us and thus glorify the Father. It is our duty to be on our guard at all times, lest we lose courage when called into the "judgment hall" to give a reason for the faith that is in us. We must see that our fellowship is able to stand the test in every trial so that no one can point the finger of scorn at us and say, "Hypocrite, even your words condemn you!" It is our duty, yea, our privilege, "To make all men see what is the fellowship of the mystery, which from the beginning of the world hath been hid in God,"[18] and now is being revealed.

Fellowship Brings a Peace That Passes Understanding

As we have dealt with our fellow human beings, we may expect to be dealt with. What cause have we for fear if we have obeyed the Voice? We have become as little children putting our trust in the Giver of all good and perfect gifts, and we know that He will reward us according to His goodness and mercy. "Great peace have they which love Thy law; and nothing shall offend them."[19]

To whom do we look for this peace? Who hath brought the Pleiades into being, or set the bands of Orion, or the waters of the deep that are cast upon the land, or brings breath into the life of all His creatures and supplies the union with those Creative Forces that makes for the songs of the spheres? The Lord is His name. Under the shadow of His wing there is peace and no cause for fear. (See 262-23.)

Let nothing stand between us and the Father, but rather let us cast aside the things that have hindered in the past and allow no care to weigh us down as we go forth in His name day by day. Do we not know and are we not confident that "All things work together for good to them that love God, to them who are the called according to his purpose"?[20] There may be things we do not

[17]Matt. 16:18   [18]Eph. 3:9   [19]Psalm 119:165   [20]Romans 8:28

understand now, but those things we can safely leave in the hands of the Father, knowing that He will reveal them in His own good time. Let no worry or condemnation enter our minds that might hinder the fellowship we have with the Father. The time is at hand. "He that is unjust, let him be unjust still; and he which is filthy, let him be filthy still; and he that is righteous, let him be righteous still; and he that is holy, let him be holy still."[21] It is not for us to judge, but to work, to serve, and to rely wholly on the promises: "Lo, I am with you alway, even unto the end of the world."[22] "Peace I leave with you, my peace I give unto you ... Let not your heart be troubled, neither let it be afraid."[23]

Let our meditation and prayer be expressed in the following words:

How excellent is Thy name in the earth, O Lord! Would I have fellowship with Thee, I must show brotherly love to my fellow man. Though I come in humbleness and have aught against my brother, my prayer, my meditation, does not rise to Thee. Help Thou my efforts in my approach to Thee. *262-21*

---

[21]Rev. 22:11   [22]Matt. 28:20   [23]John 14:27

Lesson VII

PATIENCE

"In your patience possess ye your souls."   Luke 21:19

Affirmation

How gracious is Thy presence in the earth, O Lord! Be Thou the guide, that we with patience may run the race which is set before us, looking to Thee, the Author, the Giver of light.

262-24

VII

PATIENCE

[Based on Edgar Cayce readings 262-24 through 262-26]

Introduction

God is the God of patience. All nature declares this. It is written in the rocks, the caverns, the hills, and the valleys—yea, deep in the heart of the earth. It is no less written in the souls of people by Him who has shown Himself to be long-suffering, forbearing, and willing, though it takes ages, for all to come to the knowledge of the light.

Patience is an activity of the God-mind within each soul. Its expression involves mental, physical, and spiritual thought and action. Through patience we learn to know self, to measure and test our ideals, to use faith, and to seek understanding through virtue. Thus all spiritual attributes are embraced in patience.

As we exercise patience day by day, we know how well we have put into activity the lessons learned from past experiences. Patience puts all the virtues into action. With patience we become channels of blessings to others —serving not in our way, but in His way—not once, but as long as there is need of service.

Value of Patience

Patience is a test of our development. Manifested in our daily lives, it shows whether we have used or abused the opportunities presented during former experiences. What great understanding results when we exercise this attribute!

It is through patience that we get a better understanding of the Father and His relationship to His children. It is through patience that we get a better understanding of the crosses that we bear day by day.

One that is without crosses has ceased to be of notice and is no longer among the children. We may be called upon to bear not only our own crosses but those of others. If we would approach the Throne, we must come leaning upon the arm of a neighbor we have helped. This manifests our relationship to each other.

Patience, as nothing else, shows growth. We often find ourselves so able to meet some difficult problems that we feel we have solved them before. Doubtless we have, again and again. At other times we are not able to cope with problems not nearly so intricate. Why do we have such experiences? If we fail in meeting these in the right spirit and find ourselves beaten, do we not act the parts of weaklings? As we realize our mistakes, we become ashamed that we lost hold of ourselves, and resolve that we will profit by the mistakes. Because of these experiences, we should ever afterwards count ourselves happy to endure, and be more willing to wait until we are better understood, and until we can better understand. It is the lessons learned through patience that in the end strengthen and help us; then we become examples to others. Something, too, has taken place within us, for something is written that the hand of time cannot efface. We have found a pearl of great price to be set in the soul, where it will remain through all eternity!

How kind is the wise provision of the Father! He gives to us each moment just what we are able to use. We cannot use aright that which we do not understand. "I have yet many things to say unto you, but ye cannot bear them now."[1] As we do our bit to make His promises real by showing our neighbors that we understand their burdens and are ready to help them bear them, we become more and more able to know the love of the Father and more conscious of our own growth.

The beauty of the soul shows in the life of individuals who have patience. This comes to those who have a constant, prayerful attitude for a purposeful life. In order to have this beauty of the soul's expression, it is necessary that we forget ourselves. It is not altogether an outward growth but an inward one, too. It is the result of introspection, which is the foundation of deep meditation. Love is manifested in every word and act, even as it was in those of the Master. So, through patience let us magnify His attributes

[1]John 16:12

in our experiences. There is nothing to regret in exercising patience—there is everything, in the loss of it. We are building for eternity. Results do not always manifest at once.

One individual relates the following experience: "I was called upon to pass through a great trial. My supply of patience and endurance seemed to become more and more depleted as the days went by. Beginning to realize, at last, that I was only an instrument—a channel through which God's will was being manifested—my strength and courage gradually returned until, without fear, I faced the issues at stake and came to a clearer and better understanding of the problem. It was worth all to have patiently waited and to have felt His presence."

His presence with peace is the promise to us who with patience endure the crosses that are set before us day by day.

Means Through Which Patience Is Gained

In patience we become aware of our presence before the Throne. Let us seek often, then, to awaken our inner selves. With patience this may be accomplished. If we lose hold on ourselves, through the lack of patience, there is the opportunity for the entering in of those things that would make us afraid. In waiting we have the promise that His strength is sufficient for us. There is no danger of defeat, and there is no cause for fear. It is necessary, however, that we be in perfect attunement with our ideal, if we are desirous of possessing this virtue, patience, that is so necessary for our spiritual growth. There may come many harassing experiences that would seem to separate us from the Maker, but each experience has its reward. As we seek, let us know that the Comforter, who will come to us at all times, is near, and we will never be left alone.

The understanding of His laws will come, little by little, as we apply what we already know. The development of patience requires prayer and a constant watch upon ourselves, lest we be off guard and let slip an angry word or a quick retort, causing someone to stumble. Think on these things. Selfishness retards our progress in gaining patience. The recognition of this means the taking of a bold step, but a necessary one, if we would have that patience with others that we are desiring for ourselves. Lose self in Him; find self in service. Lose self in Him; find self one with the Father. The step is magic, the realization divine, when every act, every thought, and every word is so actuated by the spirit of patience that others will endeavor to emulate our example. This becomes the natural experience to the heart that recognizes God in everyone.

In the trials that arise day by day, our patience is tested. We begin to grow as we overcome and put behind us each new obstacle. Passive submission will not suffice; our patience must be an active, growing force which rises to meet each new trial. Whom the Lord loveth He chasteneth and purgeth every one, for corruption may not inherit eternal life, but must be burned up. Let us know that our God is a consuming fire and must purge everyone that would be one with Him.[2]

We overcome only through patience. We develop by pressing on, by expending spiritual energy, and in so doing we open the way for God to lend the sustaining strength of His presence in times of trial and tests that come to all.

How may we more perfectly live the life that we may through patience gain the better understanding? By applying what we know day by day. The Spirit does not call on us to live what we do not already know and understand. In doing there comes the knowledge and the understanding for the next step. When should we begin? Today, for "Now is the accepted time,"[3] we read. Let us enter in through faith and with patience wait for the next step. Those of us who make ourselves unworthy of being tried are unworthy of being trusted for the entering in.

It Takes Patience to Run the Race

The trying of our faith worketh patience,[4] we are told in Scripture. Day by day, step by step, the race is run. When we think our patience is entirely exhausted, then we have lost patience with ourselves. What a hell it becomes if we become impatient with ourselves! How quickly we must hasten to analyze ourselves and make the necessary corrections and adjustments! Influences from within are stronger than from without; thus our higher selves stand ready to help, if we are really anxious to set ourselves right. What an opportunity for growth and a closer approach to Him! Let us live just today, as if the race were ended, the work completed—as if upon this day's endeavors depended

[2]See Hebrews 12:6; I Cor. 15:50; Deut. 4:24   [3]II Cor. 6:2   [4]See James 1:3

the fulfillment of all of His promises. If we expected the Master, the Christ, to dine with us today, what would we have to offer as the fruits of our lives, our thoughts, our acts, or our deeds?

Patience is a virtue that has no vacation. How watchful we must be, lest malice or censure creep in, and we lose everything for which we have striven! We are called upon at all times to lay aside those things that hinder, and to run with patience the race set before us. The race must be run, for it is the way back to the Father. Let us be thankful that we do not have to run alone. "I am the way . . . no man cometh unto the Father, but by me."[5] Only the activity of patience, with trust in Him, will enable us to meet all trying conditions and rise above each new barrier.

Personal Experiences

"When I have gained an understanding of true cooperation necessary for each activity and have lost sight of self in service, then I have the knowledge of His presence abiding within, and more and more I express patience—the patience that feeds my soul. I can walk and work and wait peacefully in Spirit and know all is well!"

Patience is the chief cornerstone of soul development. It is, moreover, the watch set at the gateway leading from the physical body to the soul. With it we not only meet the weaknesses of ourselves, but are able to estimate the strength found in developing various attributes of the soul—love, faith, and hope. What we are, what we have been, and what we intend to be are shown more in the patience we exhibit than through any other virtue. It shows just how we have stood the tests in the past: how we have met and conquered them, or gone down in defeat before them. Patience shows just what our development is: whether we are ready to bear with others and overlook their shortcomings, or are primitive in thinking that our way is the only way to truth and real understanding.

"In your patience possess ye your souls!"[6] "For what shall it profit a man, if he shall gain the whole world, and lose his own soul? Or what shall a man give in exchange for his soul?"[7] When we possess this priceless gift, received from the hands of the Father, shall we, in order to assert our rights, pay so high a price that we would give our soul in exchange for self-aggrandizement?

There may be much to bear before we can have the title to the

[5]John 14:6   [6]Luke 21:19   [7]Mark 8:36, 37

possession cleared in our minds, but through patience in each trial we become stronger for the next. The Master was asked, "How oft shall my brother sin against me and I forgive him—till seven times?"[8] The reply was, "I say not ... until seven times, but until seventy times seven!" Is seventy times seven built within us? Are we ready to bear and forbear until the end, or ready to give insult for insult, blow for blow? Are we not, by our lack of self-control, showing only how far we are failing to measure up to the standard we have set for others? Much is buried deep within these souls of ours, much that we should know. As we more and more exercise patience and put into practice what we know, we will grow in grace, knowledge, and understanding. Lord, direct us in the patience of the Christ!

As we understand more perfectly what it means to be a channel of blessings to others and become more aware of the presence of the Father, greater patience will find a place in our lives.

"Be patient; stablish your hearts, for the coming of the Lord draweth nigh,"[9] we are instructed. When? This is the time—today. The time draws nigh for each of us to become more aware of the necessity of magnifying His presence through the patience we have with our fellow humans, in order that He may be glorified in us through the promise of the Father. For "Inasmuch as ye have done it unto the least of these, my little ones, ye have done it unto Me."[10]

Then let our prayer be expressed in these words:

> How gracious is Thy presence in the earth, O Lord! Be Thou the guide, that we with patience may run the race which is set before us, looking to Thee, the Author, the Giver of light.
>
> *262-24*

---

[8]Matt. 18:21   [9]P.R. See James 5:8   [10]P.R. See Matt. 25:40, 45

Lesson VIII

THE OPEN DOOR

"Behold, I stand at the door, and knock; if any man hear my voice, and open the door, I will come in to him, and will sup with him, and he with me."   Revelation 3:20

Affirmation

As the Father knoweth me, so may I know the Father, through the Christ Spirit, the door to the kingdom of the Father. Show Thou me the way.   *262-27*

VIII

THE OPEN DOOR

[Based on Edgar Cayce readings 262-27 through 262-30]

Why shrinkest thou, my soul?
Doth thou not know new strength comes but by faith
And faith renewed, and effort newly made?
And couldst thou even dare to hope to catch
The faintest glimpse of the Ineffable,
If thou doth not stretch out to thy full length
The helping hand to open wide the door?

[By Mrs. 2118 for this lesson]

Introduction

The kingdom of God, the glory of the oneness in the Infinite, is the eternal destiny of every soul, the ultimate goal of every entity, regardless of his or her place or position in the seemingly complex scheme of things. In each there is felt that urge to press on. Through ignorance and misunderstanding many seek only the gratification of selfish desires, fighting, struggling, as it were, against the inflexible laws which an all-wise Creator has set. Eventually, each struggling soul must face the realities of life and make his or her will one with that of the divine Maker. With this comes peace in the realization of "I and my Father are one."[1]

The door to the kingdom of the Father is through the life, the Spirit of the life, manifested in the Christ Consciousness in the material world. It is opened only by the efforts of an individual. Throughout the previous lessons, continual emphasis has been placed upon the awakening of the Christ Consciousness. Each lesson has presented some attribute of the soul, some faculty of the inner self, which, if magnified in the conscious activities of

[1]John 10:30

81

the individual day by day, will add to and strengthen the growth
of the soul's expression through the physical person. May we not
ask these questions? Who, then, of us has learned to be truly
cooperative one with another? Who has learned oneself sufficiently
to know wherein one stands in relation to one's fellow human
beings? Who has set the ideal wholly in Him? Who has magnified
the faith in the Father and in the Son, that it may be accounted
to that one for righteousness? Who has virtue and understanding?
Who has fellowship with the Father? Who has in patience
possessed one's own soul?

The Christ Spirit comes as a result of Christ-like action. To
each it comes as a realization of the activity of the soul forces. As
the creative urge stirs the seed of the flower, just so the activity
of the soul expressed through cooperation, a knowledge of self,
the ideal set in Him, faith, virtue, understanding, and patience
stirs an individual, and there is upward growth. As the flower in
due time blossoms forth, just so the soul of humanity, through
the Christ Spirit, comes into its full power and glory.

The Preparation of Self

The preparation for the way is a preparation of self. Each of us
is the door that He, the Way, may enter. "Behold, I stand at the
door, and knock."[2] "I am the way, the truth, and the life."[3] We
must work to bring that consciousness, that awareness of His
presence, into our material and mental affairs of life. The lesson
must ever be, the spirit is the life, the mind is the builder, and the
physical is the result.

Only when we completely surrender to the working of the
Christ Spirit, can we say truthfully the door to the kingdom
within is open. All selfish thoughts must be obliterated and
replaced with the desire to be used by Him in carrying out His
will in the world. When we seek our neighbor's good, rather than
our own, we may expect our reward in proportion to the good we
send out. When we become self-centered, we eventually feel that
we are being cheated in life. It is then that we close ourselves to
the good we might give out, and at the same time, build a barrier
to the good that might flow to us.

As we seek to know the way, we must come in singleness of
purpose and think not of the hindrances that are made by

²Rev. 3:20   ³John 14:6

mortals; rather, know in whom we have believed and recognize that He has brought all things into being. As we seek and know this, we are His. In choosing Him, He has chosen us. As we realize we are one with Him, we become workers, pointing others to that joy, peace, and happiness that we have found. Will we not be faithful to the calling wherein He has called us?

How shall we begin? Let us take that which we have in hand, that which we have builded day by day, and, without fear, open the door that He may enter in and abide with us. Faith is the beacon that lights the path to the open door of the Father's house. Service is the password that admits us into the banquet hall. Come ye blessed of my Father, enter into the Kingdom prepared for you—for as ye have done unto one of the least of these, My brethren, so ye did it unto Me.[4]

We have to contend with many conflicting forces when we would have faith and serve others. Selfishness and sensitiveness shut the Ideal from view and prevent a wholehearted cooperation with our fellow human beings in our daily lives. They may so retard our development that nothing seems worthwhile. These hindering qualities can even bring thoughts of self-destruction. It is only when self is put aside and the Spirit is allowed to lead that we indeed are free and able to accomplish anything that is of real, lasting value. When the thoughts of doubt, lack, and self-condemnation begin to creep in, the door begins to close more and more, until not even a ray of light may filter through to light the way. When these thoughts are allowed to remain in control, there is no despair more terrible. We are shutting out the light and living behind closed doors—closed to God and His goodness. Do we wonder, that where these thoughts are uppermost there are suicides, murders, and sins of every kind in evidence? Are not many in the world at this time ready to be shown a more perfect way? We show through service that as He overcame the world and became the Way, just so may we, who follow in His steps, overcome all things.

How to Open the Door

We must open the door if we would have the Christ enter. As we, with the Christ Consciousness as the standard, manifest His love in our daily walks in and before others, so we open the door.

[4]See Matt. 25:40

Then it is that we heed the call to the Spirit within that stands ever ready to commune with us. It does not come in the whirlwind, but as a still, small Voice. If we listen and trust, it will teach us all things and bring all things to our remembrance.

If we would recognize this great Intelligence, this great I AM that knocks for admission into every heart, then let us heed these words: "Ye that have named the Name, make known in thy daily walks, in thy acts, the lessons that have been builded in meditation and prayer."[5]

Good rulers will continually seek a contact with their subjects that they may understand their needs, and they will be quick to reward any special obedience to the laws. How much greater will the Heavenly Father, who watches over His children, be ready to help them! Yet, God requires that we seek His face and believe that He is, before He reveals Himself. We must make the effort, if we wish to open the door to His Kingdom. "If ye will be my people, I will be your God."[6]

What is the way to the Father? It is through the Christ (having the Christ Consciousness) that we come to the Father, open the door, see the way, and hear His voice. When we close our ears to the pleadings of the less fortunate, we close the door to His presence; for in so doing we do not manifest the mind of the Christ. "When saw we Thee naked and clothed Thee, hungry and fed Thee, a stranger and took Thee in? Inasmuch as ye did it unto one of the least of these little ones, ye did it unto Me."[7] Let us know that when we speak a kind word or lighten the care of a neighbor, we open the door that He may enter, and through Him is the way into the Father's Kingdom, and there is no other.

As we seek to magnify His Spirit, let us know that we, too, become doors through which others may be drawn into the way. We are living in a material world of three dimensions; the spirituality that we wish to reflect must be expressed in and through material thought and activity, if we sincerely desire to reach and to awaken others. What is to be gained if we shout from the housetop concerning love for others and forget the little acts of kindness or the smiles that will lighten others day by day?

When we are aware of the Christ Consciousness within, we begin to put into action the Christ Spirit without. It is only in the application of our spiritual attributes day by day that we become

[5]P.R. [6]P.R. See Hebrews 8:10; Lev. 26:12; Jer. 30:22 [7]P.R. See Matt. 25:38, 40

living examples, showing our at-onement with Him; thus, we not only open the door, but as channels, are doors. Let us not forget, as we work, that those we meet along the way are seekers also and are the Israel of the Lord.

How to Know the Father

As the Father knoweth us, so we may know the Father. The Father judges us in our relationships to our fellow human beings. As we give, so we receive; as we measure, so it is meted to us; as we forgive, so we are forgiven—not because the Father wills it, but because we have chosen it to be so by our own acts, words, and deeds. It is the Father's good pleasure to give to each nothing less than the kingdom. Would we know the Father? Let us then stretch out our hands in love and sympathy to our faltering neighbors, and as we lift them up, so shall we even then in that hour be lifted up. Acknowledge each in his or her respective sphere of development, for that is the necessary stage of experience. Let us remember that Zaccheus climbed higher that he might have a broader vision, and on that day dined with Truth.

We know the Father by exemplifying His attributes in the earth. Let us not hope to reach all in a day, but little by little, line upon line, precept upon precept, here a little, there a little, until we come daily to know more and more of the Father.

As we lose ourselves in Him, earnestly desiring to put into practice the prayer, "Not my will, but Thine, O Lord, be done in and through me,"[8] we realize our oneness with the Christ, the door to the kingdom of the Father. We will find that the Father is not an arbitrary master, one who is demanding our service, but an all-wise Provider, a Father who understands all our needs. This was understood by the Psalmist when he sang, "O how I love thy law! It is my meditation all the day."[9] We will get a new concept of the Father the moment we make His will our own.

The Great Need for Service

We are our neighbor's keeper. A new revelation is taking place. A new order of things is being born. Old things are passing away and, behold, new things are about to appear. We are considering our relationship to our fellow humans as never before. Let us

[8]Mark 14:36   [9]See Psalm 119:97

catch more clearly the note of compassion and love taught by our Elder Brother and, in His Spirit, pass it on. Let us not sit and wait until tomorrow, but use that opportunity, that privilege, and that promise today. Let selfishness be swallowed up in selflessness.

There is a great need for service. A stream that has no outlet becomes stagnant and impure. Self-development is not the whole purpose of service. There is a greater need. We must see to it that our neighbor, too, comes to the knowledge of the Light. There are responsibilities as well as joys in service. Storms may come, but it is He who stills the tempest for us. He brings rest to those who are tired. No matter what the trials may be, keep the faith. Let self be as naught that He, the Guide and Leader, may be better understood by those who look to our activities. He is the Light, and as we walk closer to Him the way becomes brighter.

If we would be channels, we must demonstrate in our lives what we teach. Let us choose each day some truth, live it first for self, then for others, that they may see our good works as we put into practical operation just what we say we believe and teach. It will work. The Master said, "Lo, I am with you alway, even unto the end of the world."[10]

The Kingdom of the Father

To be aware of the Christ Consciousness within is to open the way for the Christ Spirit to manifest in our lives. The way is open to all who seek. The trials may be many, but through the Christ Spirit we are able to meet them. There is a consciousness of His force, power, and activity upon which we may draw. When doubts arise, it is a call to prayer. Let no doubt linger, but give thanks that it is only a look onward and upward that will again restore the faith upon which our hope is built.

The possession of an earthly kingdom is worth the seeking of a lifetime. There is not only responsibility but honor in its possession. There is a certain satisfaction that something is being accomplished by self and, perhaps, for others. How much greater is a possession in the kingdom of the Father—that kingdom prepared for us from the foundation of the world. What can stand in our way? Only self! As we realize this, may we not push self aside and let the Spirit lead us fully into that possession

[10]Matt. 28:20

which is our birthright, and thereby exercise the benediction of Him who said, "All power is given unto me in heaven and in earth"?[11]

Be still, my children! Bow thine heads that the Lord of the Way may make known unto you that have been chosen for a service in this period when there is the need of that Spirit being made manifest in the earth, that the way may be known to those that seek the Light! For the glory of the Father will be made manifest through you that are faithful unto the calling wherein ye have been called! Ye that have named the Name make known in thy daily walks of life, in the little acts of the lessons that have been builded into your own experience, through those associations of self in meditation and prayer, that His way may be known among men. For He calls on all—whosoever will may come—and He stands at the door of your own conscience, that ye may be aware that the Scepter has not departed from Israel, nor have His ways been in vain: For today, will ye harken, the way is open—I, Michael, call on thee!

262-27

Bow thine heads, O ye sons of men, would ye know the Way: For I, Michael, the Lord of the Way, would warn ye that thou standest not in the way of thy brother nor sittest in the seats of the scornful, but rather make known that love, that glory, that power in His Name, that none be afraid: for I, Michael, have spoken!

262-28

Hark! O ye children of men! Bow thine heads, ye sons of men: For the glory of the Lord is thine, will ye be faithful to the trust that is put in each of you!

Know in whom ye have believed! Know that He is Lord of all, and His word faileth not to them that are faithful, day by day: for I, Michael, would protect those that seek to know His face!

262-29

Let our prayer be expressed in these words:

As the Father knoweth me, so may I know the Father, through the Christ Spirit, the door to the kingdom of the Father. Show Thou me the way.

262-27

[11]Matt. 28:18

Lesson IX

IN HIS PRESENCE

"And I will walk among you, and will be your God, and ye shall be my people." Leviticus 26:12

Affirmation

Our Father who art in heaven, may Thy kingdom come in earth through Thy presence in me, that the light of Thy word may shine unto those that I meet day by day. May Thy presence in my brother be such that I may glorify Thee. May I so conduct my own life that others may know Thy presence abides with me, and thus glorify Thee.   *262-30*

IX

IN HIS PRESENCE

[Based on Edgar Cayce readings 262-31 through 262-34]

"Lift up your heads, O ye gates;
And be ye lift up, ye everlasting doors,
And the King of glory shall come in."[1]

Introduction

Our thoughts, our words, our activities, and our general outlook on life are motivated by our concept of Him whom we worship. Our inner life and reaction to all environs and associations are expressions of what we have done about or with the knowledge and consciousness of His presence abiding with us.

When we keep His presence as a thing apart, something to be experienced or something of which to be aware, then, when we are disturbed in some manner, we lose sight of the fact that to abide in His presence can be the experience, the knowledge, and the understanding of all who seek to do His bidding. His presence abides with us always, for it is in Him we live and move and have our being. We must realize this, and come to know and understand that we are children of God.

God is Spirit, standing back of everything in creation. God is One. We cannot separate Him from His creation. We may try to do so, but in so doing we become dual, mystified, and confused. When we separate ourselves or think ourselves apart from our Maker, we are like ships without rudders.

The oneness is ever existent, but it is only through our realization and our acknowledgment of its existence that the change is worked in us, and life takes on a new aspect. We are free-will agents. God is not a person in the sense that we think

[1]Psalm 24:7

of persons; yet, to those of us who seek His presence, He is very personal. He is God to all—Father, to those who seek.

It is our oneness with the Father that the Master stressed while on earth in a physical body, when He declared that He could do nothing of Himself: It was the Father within Him that did the works. Just so we, to do the works of God, must seek ever to be conscious of the Presence within. All the guidance, help, supply, joy, peace, and whatever goes to make life worth living is within. "Seek, and ye shall find; knock, and it shall be opened unto you."[2]

Know, O ye children, the Lord thy God is One. Each spirit, each manifestation—either in this or any other sphere of development—moves toward the knowledge, the understanding, and the conception of that One—Him, God, Jehovah, Yah—the All One.

It is only when we listen to the still small voice within and know that His presence is with us that we come to the realization that we are one with Him.

The Knowledge of His Presence

It is within the human soul, the simplest unit of God (which we would make complex), that we will find Him abiding. Sensing the presence of God within and without, we become quiet, throw off anxiety, and are conscious of a renewing power. The Spirit of God speaks through the soul—the soul forces. How may we know this? We must study and meditate until we realize what attitude we hold concerning His presence. People of old have said, "Such knowledge is too wonderful for me; it is high, I cannot attain unto it."[3] We, too, may feel at times that it is physically impossible to attain to that knowledge. May we not take God at His word and accept His free gift of grace, love, and mercy? "If any of you lack wisdom, let him ask of God, that giveth to all men liberally, and upbraideth not."[4] "I am the Lord. I change not."[5]

We obscure the knowledge of His presence by considering it as a thing apart. Let us not quench the spirit within. As His spirit bears witness with our spirit, not only will we understand ourselves better, but there will come a fuller understanding of our neighbor, our friend, or our enemy. As we go fearlessly on into whatever work is before us, let us trust in His care, knowing that

[2]Luke 11:9   [3]Psalm 139:6   [4]James 1:5   [5]Mal. 3:6

His presence will overshadow us. The Light will shine ahead and show the way. He will keep our stumbling feet from faltering and will allow no harm to overtake us. May we live each moment aware of His presence and let our work testify for us.

As self is less and less magnified and more hope and reliance is sought in His Word, each of us will become more and more aware of His abiding presence. All who would know Him must believe that He is, and that He is a rewarder of those who diligently seek Him. How often have we read, "The Lord is my shepherd,"[6] and doubted the truth of it as applying to us. By submitting our will to divine guidance we come step by step into the realization that He will withhold no good thing from those who seek Him, who seek to do His will.

The Preparation of Self

The realization that we are ever in His presence is not always easy when we allow the cares of the world to creep in and draw us away in body and mind. As we are in various stages of growth, so we are in different states of consciousness. What might be absolutely necessary for the preparation of self for one of us, for another might be secondary. It is well, however, for all to observe:

1. The laws of righteous judgment and clean living.
2. Special hours for meditation and prayer, that we may be strengthened during times of severe temptation and trials.
3. The realization that He is ever with us, whether we are in sorrow or joy, for mind is the builder.
4. Such standards of conduct that others may know that what we profess with our lips to believe is in keeping with that which we hold as our ideal.

We should be living examples of what we profess. Many of us follow from afar and our actions are not in keeping with the Christ Consciousness. We often give others the wrong impression of His attributes manifesting through us.

"If ye love me, keep my commandments."[7] What are His commandments? "Inasmuch as ye have done it unto one of the least of these my little ones, ye have done it unto me."[8] "I will come again, and receive you unto myself; that where I am [in consciousness], there ye may be also."[9]

6Psalm 23:1   7John 14:15   8P.R. See Matt. 25:40   9John 14:3

Finally, as we abide in His presence, though there may come trials of every kind, and though tears may flow from the breaking up of the carnal forces within, the spirit is made glad, even as He in the hour of trial smiled upon him by whom He was denied.

Let us remember that physically, mentally, and spiritually we continually reflect our understanding of His presence. Let us study to show ourselves approved unto Him day by day; for in so doing the light of His presence shows forth in our precepts, in our examples, in our words, and in our works.

As we look upon our fellow humans, we find that their activities, in whatever sphere they may be, are expressions of the attitudes they have builded regarding God. Their life reflects what they worship. Their actions show the spirit which is within them. Are they not using the same measure for us?

In the physical body, good health is a reflection of our observance of physical laws. Even the small details involving the care of the body are important, for they are either in accord with laws that bring a finer type of expression or lead to inharmony. The physical surroundings, the type of companions sought, and every physical action express to others our concept of how near God, law, and love are to us.

As the activities of the body reflect the strength of the physical person, so the activities of the mind reflect the strength of the mental body. The question of controlling our actions physically is in part answered by laws and customs made by mortals; but the problems of controlling our thoughts, which truly may be just as harmful and out of tune with the Infinite, are personal matters which must be met by each individual. Thought vibrations go out, words are spoken, deeds are done, and all carry to others their influences and their impressions of our understanding of God.

How spiritual are our lives? How often do we seek through meditation and prayer contacts with our Creator? Do our attitudes and our philosophies of life center about a spiritual ideal? Others look for these signs and are influenced by them. We believe, but do we express our belief in our words, thoughts, deeds, and attitudes?

Experiencing the Abiding Presence

The consciousness that He walks and talks with us, and that His promises are ever present, brings abiding peace. This makes for joy in service, even though it requires that there be greater and greater sacrifices of the carnal forces within our experiences. Joy does not come through service that benefits self. One that serves through kind words, thoughts, or deeds, gives of oneself, even as He, the Master.

With the realization of being in His presence comes that peace which casts out all fear and loneliness. There comes a feeling of being a part of the scheme of things. This is recognizing the God within as well as without. With this realization the way is easier. We will have more consideration for others. Condemnation will be cast aside and we will have a desire to bless.

"My presence shall go with thee, and I will give thee rest."[10] The protection of the Holy Spirit is His promise, if we are faithful. As we use what we know, not waiting for physical results before going on to the next step, we will find—when we least expect it—that which we desire has been granted. We are children in faith, knowledge, and understanding; we have to be taught and disciplined. Could a child be trusted with a live wire? No more could we be trusted with divine power until we, through love, discipline, and faith come to understand the divine law. It is the Father's good pleasure to give us the kingdom. It is ours only when we learn through patience to possess our souls.

Personal Experiences

"I was arrested on a false charge. In the presence of hardened officers of the law these words came to me: 'If God be with you, who can be against you?'[11]And then came the words of the Master, 'Be not afraid.'[12] His presence was greater than any other, and the situation, which had the material outlook of humiliation and shame, was turned to the glorifying of His name in the earth. My awareness of the great need of His presence made me more conscious of it. In Him we do, indeed, live and move and have our being. Each thought, word, and act is an opportunity to advertise His presence. Let us then be an advertisement for God."

"I was asked to give a talk in public. The request came so

[10]Exodus 33:14   [11]Romans 8:31   [12]Mark 6:50

suddenly that I had no opportunity to prepare myself. I was tempted to devote my period for meditation to study the subject, but the Spirit forbade, assuring me He that is within is greater than he that is without. I harkened and with scarcely a thought appeared before the congregation. Never had I felt so keenly the presence of the Spirit as on this occasion. The words came without effort. I felt that there was a message of helpfulness, inspiration, and power being given through me. It was not I, but the Spirit within, that was doing the work. Others bore witness that the message was to them one above the ordinary, not only in words, but in power, and in presentation. Surely, we are strong when we acknowledge our own weakness and rely on the Presence within. It is only when we forget God that troubles overtake us. If we today, at this time of testing, would place our hope of deliverance in the hands of the Father instead of humankind, we would not fail to come out more than conquerors."

"There is within me a knowledge that His presence abides with me always as a part of me, not apart from me. Through the toil of the day, through the quiet hours of the night, He is always near. When burdens of the material life are heavy, if I stop and listen, He assures me that He is with me."

Let Us Remember That Our Guard Is Ever in His Presence

Let us not be afraid in the presence of our Maker. He is willing to fulfill His promises to His children and ready to make known His ways unto those who will seek His face. The God who wrought the beauties of nature and set the laws which govern the harmonious symphony of the universe could not have left a part of His creation without guidance or without a sustaining force. The way is exemplified in the Son, and there are those universal Forces ever ready to aid and strengthen those who seek to travel this way.

Bow thine heads, O ye men that would seek His presence. Be strong in His might. Falter not at thy own weak self. Know that thy Redeemer liveth and may this day make known in thy own heart His presence abiding with thee. Root from thy body, thy consciousness, aught that would hinder His entering in, for He would sup with thee. Wilt thou then, O man, make known thine own decisions? Will ye be one with Him? The way which I guard leads to that of glory in the might of the Lord. I, Michael, would guide thee. Do not disobey. Do not falter. Thou knowest the way.   *262-33*

Let us glory in the Lord, not in self, and not in the wisdom of the earth—knowing that those who partake alone of the mental may easily become stumbling stones in the way of many. Let the Spirit of Truth that is within separate the chaff from the wheat, that we may enter into the full knowledge of His presence, and shut out those things that would hinder or cause doubt or in any way make us afraid. (See 262-32.)

Let this be our prayer:

> Our Father who art in heaven, may Thy kingdom come in earth through Thy presence in me, that the light of Thy word may shine unto those that I meet day by day. May Thy presence in my brother be such that I may glorify Thee. May I so conduct my own life that others may know Thy presence abides with me, and thus glorify Thee.   *262-30*

Come! Let our hearts be lifted in praise and adoration of the wondrous love that the Father sheds upon the children of men.

Come! Let all be glad in the opportunities that are given to serve in His name day by day.

Come! Let us be joyful in the truth that "Inasmuch as ye did it unto the least of these my little ones, ye did it unto me."[13] Let the love of the Son be magnified in our lives that others may know that the joyousness of service brings peace and harmony to our hearts as we serve.

Come! Give thanks unto Him, for we would make our own lives and our own bodies a dwelling place of the love that the Father would manifest unto His children.

Come! Give place to His Holy Name that there may come joyousness in the hearts of all at the coming of the Christ into the lives and the experiences of many. (See 281-14.)

[13]Matt. 25:40

Lesson X

THE CROSS AND THE CROWN

"Fear none of those things which thou shalt suffer: Behold, the devil shall cast some of you into prison, that ye may be tried; and ye shall have tribulation ten days: Be thou faithful unto death, and I will give thee a crown of life."   Revelation 2:10

Affirmation

Our Father, our God, as we approach that that may give us a
better insight of what He bore in the cross, what His glory may
be in the crown, may Thy blessings—as promised through Him—
be with us as we study together in His name.   *262-34*

X

THE CROSS AND THE CROWN

[Based on Edgar Cayce readings 262-34 through 262-38]

Introduction

"And ye shall know the truth,
and the truth shall make you free."[1]

If we come to understand these lessons and that to which they
are leading, and if we hope to lead others in the way, we will find
it necessary to analyze ourselves as to that which is, which has
been, and which may be the impelling influence in our lives. We
must discard everything that bespeaks selfishness or the
magnifying of those desires that are gratifying only to the carnal
influences in our lives.

In previous lessons, truths which could be applied in anyone's
daily life have been presented. In studying this lesson, "The
Cross and the Crown," we have the opportunity to take a definite
stand, if we accept the following decision as our own: "For I
determined not to know anything among you, save Jesus Christ,
and him crucified."[2]

Do we feel that the cross represents something very definite in
the life of each of us in our activities through the earth? The
Christ Spirit has led in the presentation of truth in every age, in
every clime, and came at last to the cross. He triumphed over
death, hell, and the grave.

We choose this way not in an attitude of narrow-mindedness,
but with a glimpse of the freedom which it brings—embodying,
as it does, the light and truth of the eternal and universal Spirit
of the divine Creator.

Let us pause as we take up the study of this lesson and each

[1]John 8:32   [2]I Cor. 2:2   101

of us ask ourselves this question: "Why have I chosen the way of the cross?" To troubled minds and tired hearts the way seems long and hard. Bypaths and shortcuts beckon invitingly, but the eternal self cannot be hushed for long with the things that satisfy not, for it urges ever onward toward the Everlasting. In passing through various experiences in the earth plane we come at last to recognize and accept His way, the way of service, the way of sacrifice, and the way of selflessness. We come to realize that there is no other way to attain our ultimate goal except the one trod by Him who made the supreme sacrifice that we might find our way back to the Father. We come to realize that, in fact, there is no other name given among us whereby we can be saved from self except through Him. The way of the cross which He chose will lead us out of our dissolution and into the light of understanding of our true purpose in the world; then the cross becomes a symbol of that which must be borne and overcome in every life. It is natural that as we study, the purpose of our trials becomes more apparent. We begin to realize that we must overcome if we would go on; those things in our hearts that hinder our progress must be torn out and cast aside. This is not easy to do without His help. He, having gone all the way, understands all our trials and temptations and, in love, willingly gives strength to us.

"I am the way, the truth, and the life."[3] In Him is all, and when accepted, the way is made so plain that we need not stumble. He is, indeed, the Light that lighteth every individual. He came into the world understanding the laws of all things visible and invisible, and demonstrated His power over all forces, even death. He showed that the way is the way of love. As we emulate His example by taking up our cross daily, our desires are more and more to help others. We take upon ourselves joyfully the cares, the troubles, and the crosses of those whom we contact in our little world. It is, we know, because of this divine love, which is thus manifested in our lives, that we can rejoice in that we are counted worthy to choose the way of the cross and suffer for His name's sake.

With our Ideal, the Christ, as the pattern, we have the satisfaction that our approach to the Father is assured. We know that His Spirit is already bearing witness with our spirit, that we are heirs and joint heirs with Him. There is a consciousness of

[3]John 14:6

His force, His power, and His activity in every element of action.

So, in bearing our crosses we overcome those conditions that would hinder us in meeting the issues of life. When this is realized, the reason for choosing the way of the cross becomes evident. Not to choose is to acknowledge a misunderstanding of the purposes of life and the way toward the realization of life eternal. Who has learned obedience otherwise than through suffering?

Why Is It Necessary to Bear a Cross? Because One Was Borne by Another?

Our crosses are of our own making now, as well as in the beginning. The world was lost in the delusion of creative thought, seeking to reverse the process of God's law and find gratification in the lower forms of vibration. Thus we are confronted daily by crosses arising from our participation in the delusion of our senses. As we meet, again and again, the seeds we have sown, we come to realize that it is only through overcoming them that we can ever hope to reach again the estate from which we have fallen. Rebirth is the opportunity given to the children of men by which this may be accomplished. Each life stands out, crowned with an opportunity to develop through overcoming, and it is only through selfishness or the gratification of the carnal nature that we lose. All have sinned and come short of the glory of God. The law must be met, either through the keeping of the law ourselves as under a taskmaster, or in the way provided through Him, who took upon Himself the burden of the world.

He overcame the world through experiences. In each experience He bore a cross, reaching the final cross with all power and all knowledge. He accepted the cross, hence doing away with that so-called karma that must be met by all. The immutable law of cause and effect is evidenced today in the material, the mental, and the spiritual world; but in overcoming the world, the law, He became the law. The law, then, becomes as the schoolmaster, or the school of training. We who have named the Name are no longer under the law as law, but under mercy as in Him—for in Him, and with the desires, there may be made the coordination of all things.

In bearing the cross, the flesh is crucified that His Spirit may be made manifest in the world. Each obstacle overcome adds strength for overcoming the next. We learn to overcome all that hinders us from becoming one with Him. This is made possible in service.

It is a glorious thing to know that we are helping Him through our service to others, to make known His purpose to bring humanity back to the Father. We never lose so long as we give. God gave His only begotten Son and received back a glorified Son who had shown a world the way back to the Father. It was the Son, in whom the Father was well pleased, who gave His all, even His life for His brethren. It is necessary that we bear the cross for our own development; but it is most glorious to have the opportunity to bear the cross for the sake of Him who made the way of escape possible for us.

Why Was It Necessary That He, the Maker of Heaven and Earth, Should Bear a Cross?

The God Force became ensnared in matter and, in the first Adam, fell. It was necessary, therefore, that the God Force, the Creator, individualize Himself as an example and by overcoming the world become the Law, in order that we might know the way out. So, in the last Adam all are made alive.

He, the Maker of heaven and earth, came to earth to bear the cross that He might add His experiences and activities to ours. His purpose was and is to lead the children of men back to the realization that they are, indeed, children of God and are at one with the Father.

In His bearing the cross, "It is finished,"[4] so far as the overcoming of the flesh and worldly things is concerned. He paved the way for His followers of every age. It was necessary that He, the Son of God, the Co-worker with the Creator, come to earth to demonstrate that the flesh could be overcome—thus giving glory to the Father who had made us for His glory. He bore the cross of materiality that He might change it to the glorified cross of spirituality. He left burning in the hearts of His followers the declaration, "And I, if I be lifted up ... will draw all men unto me,"[5] and again, "He that believeth on me, the works that I do shall he do also; and greater works than these shall he do; because I go unto my Father."[6]

[4]John 19:30   [5]John 12:32   [6]John 14:12

He went all the way. He was tempted in all ways, like unto us. He was numbered with the transgressors. "He was wounded for our transgressions . . . and with His stripes we are healed,"[7] and in all He was more than a conqueror. "Greater love hath no man than this, that a man lay down his life for his friends. Ye are my friends, if ye do whatsoever I command you. Henceforth I call you not servants; for the servant knoweth not what his Lord doeth: but I have called you friends; for all things that I have heard of my Father I have made known unto you. Ye have not chosen me, but I have chosen you."[8] What was the object of the cross? For what was the supreme sacrifice? That we through His strength might come to the knowledge and understanding of the way, might be able to overcome all things, and become rulers and priests and priestesses unto God.

Again, it was His way to show to humanity what divine love could do, and how it was possible to live a perfect, blameless life with all the disintegrating influences that surround us day by day. In every period of development through the ages, He has walked and talked with people. Those who understand know that whenever there was a need for our awakening, the Son of Man entered the earth plane. The cross became the emblem of Him who offered Himself of Himself. For that cause, for that purpose came He into the world that He Himself, in overcoming the world, might gain the crown.

Why Did He Come into the World as a Man That He Might Bear a Cross?

It was through His thought and will that we took physical form. Only through the physical could the spiritual essence be aroused, awakened from its slumber, and set upon the path of spiritual progress. The question is answered: First, because of His own need to conquer the world in material manifestation, and second, because of the need of humanity for a guide, a teacher, and a saviour. The first is expressed in the following: "Though he were a Son, yet learned he obedience by the things which he suffered";[9] and the second is, "I am the way, the truth, and the life."[10]

He chose to take upon Himself the responsibility of overcoming the physical or making Himself the law through the fulfillment

[7]Isaiah 53:5   [8]John 15:13-16   [9]Hebrews 5:8   [10]John 14:6

of all requirements. By adding His experiences and activities to ours He links us with God, bringing us in a closer attunement with God and causing us to become conscious of the Oneness of all. He came to show and teach us fellowship with God through our service to others.

As a human, He knew the physical trials—doubts and fears, weaknesses and turmoils—of spiritual beings encased in material shells. He showed His ability as a human to demonstrate the possibility of humankind, as human, to bring spiritual harmony into physical vibration. He ever stressed the oneness of all force, demonstrating the direct relationship between humanity and the Creator. He came in the flesh to show that we in the flesh could become as He, God in Spirit; and taught that we may be one, even as He and the Father are one. Then this one, the Adam that first entered the world, must become the Saviour of the world. It was committed into His care. "Be thou fruitful, and multiply, and subdue the earth."[11]

Hence, the first Adam, the last Adam, was given power over the earth, and, as in each soul, the first to be conquered was self. Then all things, conditions, and elements are subject unto Him. So He became that One who was able to take the world, the earth, back to the source from whence it came. All power is given into His keeping in the earth which He has overcome. Self, death, and hell became subservient unto Him through the conquering of self. "In the beginning was the Word and the Word was with God, and the Word was God. The same was in the beginning with God."[12] The Word came and dwelt among us, the offspring of self in a material world. The Word overcame the world; hence the world became then as the servant of that One who overcame it.

Why Do We, as Individuals, Necessarily Bear Much That He Bore, and Yet Say That When Taking His Yoke upon Us the Cross Becomes Easy?

We must bear what He bore because we must travel the same way to perfection that He traveled. Along that way are experiences that all must have in order to gain the power and the knowledge of overcoming. As He took upon Himself the burden of the world, so we, in our own little world, must take upon ourselves the burdens of those about us. The yoke is easier because the burden

[11]See Genesis 1:28   [12]John 1:1-2

is lighter. He bore it all. We bear only our part. In so doing we may become conscious of our real purpose to glorify the Creator and come to know that, after all, our crosses are only misunderstandings and misapplications of His laws. To practice, not preach, demands strength, power, and faith in the Ideal. Experience alone in overcoming can give a complete understanding of what it means for another to suffer, and yet not yield—to bear and forbear, and through it all love and forgive.

His yoke is easy because His presence abides with us, protecting us and sharing the burdens that otherwise would be too heavy for us to bear. Then, too, as we come to understand the meaning of our crosses and His abiding presence, our sufferings become lessons of wisdom, our turmoils more peaceful, and we rejoice as we find ourselves growing more and more into the likeness of Him who, by the way of the cross, became the Lord of lords and the King of kings.

His presence within is ever a bulwark of reserve power that enables us to resolve to acquit ourselves as humans, to fight the battle, to win the race, and to wear the crown. (See Sam. 4:9.) Our Advocate with the Father keeps open the channel through which spiritual energy flows to us, so that we can make ourselves fit channels for passing on the truth to others. Spiritual understanding brings the knowledge that matter is the tool with which we may shape the nobler life into a likeness of the Creator. Harmony with His will, understanding, and application of His laws will bring at all times peace, not tumult; joy, not sorrow; love, not hate; and strength, not weakness. With His aid and the knowledge of His Spirit bearing witness with our spirit, the yoke that we are called upon to bear becomes, in fact, easy; and the burdens laid upon us are, indeed, light.

Does the Life Lived According to Our Own Faith, Our Own Understanding, and Our Own Walking in His Presence Explain Why Each Soul Must Bear a Cross?

As we seek to apply that learned in previous lessons dealing with attributes of the soul which should be magnified through our daily activities, we begin to realize our lack of application of those essential elements or attributes. We realize that we bear crosses because we have not yet learned to give complete expression to our soul faculties. We gradually realize how much of the inner self we have covered up, pushed aside for what we considered the more important desires of the conscious self. In so doing we have pushed ourselves further and further away from God. How well we begin to comprehend that our crosses are created by ourselves!

On the other hand, as we learn and apply these attributes of the soul, there comes joy and peace in the realization that the inner self is awakening and that it is ever on the alert to express itself through the exercising of faith, virtue, and understanding. Our relationships with others are made more perfect, and the ideal is set in Him. We see our crosses in a new light; we begin to catch a glimpse of the glory of the crown. We come to the realization of having, in truth, a part of the divine plan.

Why Has the Cross Been Chosen Rather Than Some Other Philosophy That Might Correlate the Material and Spiritual Life?

The cross is the emblem of the subjective self of the One who bore the burden of the world. It is chosen, not because of the personality of the greater teacher, Jesus the man, but because of the way to the Father made plain through Jesus the Christ. It is the symbol of the life and teachings of Him who stirred the souls of all to express in all other forms of truth. It is a part of the truth of the world and the whole truth for those who choose its standard. It answers every question of the soul that is ready for light and satisfies the longing of the innermost being. It is a symbol of the way of truth and light, universal in appeal, eternal and impelling, yet personal in application. In seeking the Divine, we have taken Jesus the Christ as our Ideal, for we find in Him the embodiment of all truth throughout the ages. Others may point the way. He said, "I am the way."[13]

Why Is the Cross, the Emblem of Shame, Necessary for Those Who Seek the Crown?

We consider a cross an emblem of shame, for innately we realize it is symbolic of opposition to God's law. As in the

[13]John 14:6

beginning, the misuse of power given unto us brought suffering in this material world. The cross is the emblem of shame to those who in the material world judge from appearance. It calls for humility, not stubbornness. It calls for suffering, not retorts. It calls for patience, not impetuosity. It calls for love of enemies, not hatred. It calls for forgiveness, not unforgiveness. All this must be borne in the cross that the crown may be laid upon the brow of the real heir, and not the usurper, who would never understand his or her subjects nor the road to true development. Who else has cleared the way for humankind and said to all, "Whosoever shall do the will of my Father which is in heaven, the same is my brother, and sister, and mother"?[14]

In bearing the cross we come to know the real meaning of the crown, the joy of completing a work, and the success that is the reward of a finished race. As we develop day by day, the idea of shame passes and there comes the joy of being one with Him in the great work of redeeming humanity. It is, indeed, an emblem of opportunity, and we come to see more and more the face of the Master reflected in each cross we bear.

The cross does not always remain the cross of shame. In the life of the Christ, the Holy One, the Son of God, it became glorified in having been overcome. Just so with us; each cross met, bravely borne, and overcome, becomes radiant with light and brings us into a more perfect understanding of the purpose of life and the glory that may be in the crown of life.

> There was a cross that fell on me with shadows dark and long
> It crowded out my sun, my light, and blotted out my song;
> But when I raised my eyes for help, I saw a Radiant One,
> That stooped to lift my heavy cross—'Twas Christ, the Blessed Son.[15]

Why Must I, as a Soul in a Material Plane, Bear a Cross?

This is a question that each of us individually should ask ourselves, and the manner in which we answer determines our spiritual status. It is the spiritual gauge of our development since the fall of humanity.

Whenever this question has been considered, many go away and walk no more in the way. "Will ye go also?"[16] Shall we not

---

[14]Matt. 12:50   [15]P.E.   [16]P.R. See John 6:67

reply, "Lord, to whom shall we go? For Thou alone hast the words of eternal life." (See 262-35.) Shall we evade the cross that is ours to bear, especially at this time when humanity is entering the greatest test period in the history of the world? The words of the prophet seem to come ringing down the ages, "Who may abide the day of His coming?"[17] Know we not that it is only those whose loins are girt about with truth? Who shall be able to abide to take this stand?

As individuals in the material plane, we must of necessity bear many things coincident with His earthly experience, and by recognizing our obligations as children of the living God, as He did, and learning from Him the lesson of meekness and lowliness of heart, we exemplify through service and sacrifice the life He lived.

Knowing that the purpose of life is to be one with the Father, we have to wait if we expect to see results in material manifestation. There is no surer way of realization than "to keep on keeping on"[18] in the way of the Christ. While our efforts may seem wrong in the eyes of everyone, there is a Power that takes hold in our extremities and adjusts every situation. As we trust that Power, our strength is renewed.

As we meet the crosses, endure the temptations, and overcome them, we become heirs and joint heirs with Him to the crown of glory. All who fulfill the purpose for which they are called bear their crosses not in sorrow, not in wailing, but in the joy of the Lord.

As a sign to us who have met our crosses and have overcome them, there comes that ability to meet other and greater crosses in the joy of the Lord, and to rejoice that we are counted worthy.

Let us enter into the service that may be our part as channels of blessings to others. In so doing we become conscious that our lives are spent in the way He would have us go, and that His presence abides with us. The door is open. Virtue and understanding find activity. Faith is renewed day by day, for we are more able to understand conditions that arise—whether from the mental, the material, or the spiritual. Access to the Father may be held as a cooperative force in whatever sphere of activity we may engage when in service to others.

It is not in times or seasons or in any place—but in every place, every day, and every hour that we may show forth His love to those we contact. By our lives others may know that He walks with us and is our friend. Upon what is the glory of the crown conditioned? Faith-ful-ness.

[17]Mal. 3:2   [18]P.R. See also 364 series and 5749 series

Lesson XI

THE LORD THY GOD IS ONE

"For there is one God; and there is none other but He."

Mark 12:32

Affirmation

As my body, mind and soul are one, Thou, O Lord, in the manifestations in the earth, in power, in might, in glory, art one. May I see in that I do, day by day, more of that realization, and manifest the more.   *262-38*

XI

THE LORD THY GOD IS ONE

[Based on Edgar Cayce readings 262-38 through 262-42]

"Thou art One, the first of every number, and the foundation of
every structure.
Thou art One, and at the mystery of Thy Oneness the wise of
heart are struck dumb,
For they know not what it is.
Thou art One, and Thy Oneness can neither be increased nor
lessened;
It lacketh naught, nor doth aught remain over.
Thou art One, but not like a unit to be grasped or counted,
For number and change cannot reach Thee.
Thou art not to be envisaged, nor to be figured thus and
thus . . . "   S.I.G.

Introduction

Unity is perhaps the most difficult truth that we have to
realize and manifest, although it is evinced all about us. Through
the mouth of His prophets, the Creator repeatedly reminded His
chosen ones, "Hear, O Israel, the Lord our God is one Lord";[1] yet
they, as other nations, would wander away and seek other gods.
In the simplest and most comprehensible way, the Creator has
revealed to His creation His power, glory, and might. "The word
is very nigh unto thee, in thy mouth and in thy heart, that thou
mayest do it."[2] It is planted not only in the heart, but "The
heavens declare the glory of God; and the firmament sheweth
His handywork. Day unto day uttereth speech, and night unto
night sheweth knowledge. There is no speech nor language,
where their voice is not heard."[3]

[1]Deut. 6:4
[2]Romans 10:8 [3]Psalm 19:1-3

113

The Manifestations of God Are One

In the universe all manifestations are of God and are one with Him. In Him they live and move and have their being. This Supreme Intelligence that moves in the earth is manifested in the tiniest molecule as perfectly as in a great planet. How wonderful to realize that there is only one force, one power, one presence, and that is God, the Father. God is Spirit. "If I ascend up into heaven, Thou art there: if I make my bed in hell, behold, Thou art there. If I take the wings of the morning, and dwell in the uttermost parts of the sea; even there shall Thy hand lead me."[4]

As a pebble tossed into a lake sends out ripples that finally reach the farthest shore, just so do our acts, whether good or bad, affect others. As in our bodies, when a member is injured, the whole suffers, so do we as individuals influence the whole of society.

Our mental, physical, and spiritual bodies must be consecrated as channels for spiritual forces, if we would fully comprehend our duty to the whole and apply ourselves in working out the purposes of God. The Father has not willed that any should perish. All may come into the knowledge of their relationship to Him. When we realize this, obstacles become stepping-stones; our enemies (hindrances and weaknesses) become means through which we may mount to higher attainments.

Amid the turmoils of the present day, if we exercise patience, faith, the attributes of God, we have unparalleled opportunities to observe the Father working through His children. It is not necessary to have some great vision or experience, but just to be kind and to perform each task cheerfully. These are things of spirit and become proofs to us and the world that "My Father worketh hitherto, and I work."[5] The only thing that can separate us from this understanding is ourselves. We alone can open or shut the door.

We should never allow ourselves to feel separate and apart from God or our fellow human beings; for what affects our neighbor on the other side of the world affects us. The people of the earth are one great family. We should love without distinction, knowing that God is in all. By making ourselves perfect channels that His grace, mercy, peace, and love may flow through us, we

---

4Psalm 139:8-10   5John 5:17

come to realize more and more the Oneness of all creation. Let us keep the heart open that the voice of Him who has called may quicken every thought and act. His ways are not hidden nor far away, but are manifested to those who will hear and see the glory of the Oneness. Through the activity of the will is the method by which each of us should prepare ourselves as channels for forces that may assist in gaining a greater concept of the Oneness of the Father in the material plane.

How We May Come into the Realization of the Oneness

We come into consciousness of the Oneness, not through any act of our own other than that we believe, trust, have faith, and come to realize that all material things are, in essence, spiritual. The Master said, "Ye are gods."[6] Does it not behoove us to take Him at His word and act the part? O, Thou who art God, present within each of us, forgive our unbelief! Let us pray for the greater realization of His presence. He is real, even as a neighbor at our side, and is faithful to keep His promises. As we are striving toward this realization, let us, moment by moment, be conscious that in every act, word, and deed His power is manifesting in and through us, and that there can be no separateness. We alone shut out the glories that may be our experiences in the realization of unity. Let us see to it that our lives, activities, thoughts, and meditations are more and more in accord with the will of the Father; for in so doing we become more Godlike and less selfish, and less of the carnal influences enter into our activities. We will then be in a position to teach others and will be on fire with the power that will manifest through us, and more and more at peace and in harmony with those experiences that are ours through our walks with Him in meditation and prayer.

How may we come into a realization of the Oneness? Take God at His word, "I am God, and beside me there is none other."[7] "Without me ye can do nothing."[8] Listen to the Voice and act upon it. Learn the lessons that nature teaches. Realize that the power within us is the God Force, the good force—although we, and we alone, through our wills may misuse it, causing it to become evil. If we will wait on the Lord, He will speak to us and will bring all things to our remembrance, even to the realization of our oneness

[6]John 10:34   [7]P.R. See Isaiah 46:9   [8]John 15:5

with Him. Strive to see God in every one as well as in every thing. Meditate, pray, listen, and believe.

The At-Onement Through Jesus, the Christ

One of the basic and essential principles of Jesus' teachings is contained in the statement, "I and my Father are one."[9] It is to His life as an example and to His explanations of the Creative Force that we may turn with a feeling of complete faith for understanding. Jesus demonstrated in a very practical manner the Oneness of God as related to each individual soul. He showed us what could be attained by an individual who was willing to make his or her will one with that of the Father. He promised us that He would make intercession for us, opening a way for all who seek to be drawn to the Father.

In the simplicity of His life and teachings, Jesus brings to our understanding the fact that God is very near to us, that He is even within our own hearts. Much of the beauty and strength of His philosophy of life lies in the personal touch, in the direct connection which He establishes between us and our Creator.

Jesus' years of ministry were spent in practical demonstration of His consciousness of the Oneness of Creative Force. His words and acts were in compliance with the law which He understood so thoroughly. Whether it was on the open hillside before the masses, or in the seclusion of some quiet grove before a select few, He was ever explaining and demonstrating the truths which He knew would make us truly free. He had walked the way and now chose to guide those who also sought a closer walk with the Creator.

Jesus learned obedience through suffering. He earned the right to be the Mediator for humankind; the right to guide those who seek in His name. If we will only follow the example He set, we will come into a realization of this truth, which He lived and taught, "The Lord our God is one Lord."[10]

As we strive to make ourselves in at-onement with Him, we must deny any other influence. He will bear us up and give us the help we need. There is power in His name. It is the symbol of attainment, understanding, and the realization of God's universal law (love). It is strength for those who are weary, peace to a troubled heart and mind. He is the Saviour to all who seek the at-onement.

[9]John 10:30   [10]Deut. 6:4

Let us strive to realize more fully and show by our practical applications that we are workers together with God—that each of us, that each of God's creatures, is filling his or her niche in the great Oneness. From our point of view, it may be a very poor expression, but God sees deeper into each heart and knows all things.

The kind old lady who offers her simple herb to relieve the pain of the little child, and the skilled physician who is giving his best to mitigate the ills of humanity are as much in at-onement with Him as the saint who, with a touch of love, opens the eyes of the blind. All are doing their part with the talent given into their keeping; all are working out their own development in their own way, which is the manifestation of His will.

The fullness of the realization of the Oneness of the Father was brought to His children when Jesus the Christ sent into the world the Holy Spirit. It is the Holy Spirit that brings to our remembrance all things.

Personal Experiences

"That the Father is One with His children has been demonstrated in my life many times, but ten years ago there was an incident that makes this truth stand out more clearly to me than anything in my experience.

"My little boy was very sick. The physicians had done all in their power to help him, but their efforts appeared fruitless.

"We were living then near a church. My son, before his illness, played and talked, day after day, with the old sexton. They grew to be great friends, and the sexton loved him very dearly. He would often speak of how the child taught him lessons of forgiveness.

"One morning during the illness the sexton came to our home and asked to see the child. We led him to the room. He took off his working gloves and laid them aside, knelt by the bed and, with upturned face, began to talk with God. A new peace came into my heart. I knew that all was well. It took this saintly old man to teach me more perfectly than I had ever realized, that the Father works with those who will let Him, and can through them perform miracles."

Ministers of state from a foreign country have all the rights of their country respected in the land to which they are an ambassador. They have the power to draw on their country for protection and in the name of their country demand it in their new home. Just so we are ambassadors in the earth, representatives of the King of kings, and while here we may claim all the power and protection of the kingdom from which we came, provided we are true representatives and are carrying out the mission for which we were sent.

The chief executive of a country can broadcast a message to his or her people. The message is for all, but only those who choose to tune in will hear it. Those who do not tune in are nonetheless a part of the whole, but their negligence indicates that they are unworthy of the interest that their chief has in them.

God has not changed. He seeks to awaken every human heart as of old. It is we who may close ourselves to the constant message of love ever in the Christ. Through prayer and meditation, we can attune ourselves to a clearer understanding and realization of His love and may receive the gift of the Spirit that would make us know, "I and my Father are one."[11]

God manifests in all He has created. Whether it be in the material plane—as demonstrated by radio; in the mental realm, as experienced through thought transference; or, in the spiritual awakening, as manifests in so-called religious experiences—all substance is one. Vibration may vary from the slow motion of matter to the invisible speed of thought. Only our points of perception and understanding change with our development. Let us realize that though we may be as one who has caught only the first glimpse of light as from the entrance of a dark cave, and who still stumbles blindly over dangerous rocks and beside deep pits, we are striving ever to reach the light of truth.

As we open our hearts to the unseen Forces that surround the throne of grace, mercy, and might, and throw about ourselves the protection found in the thought of the Christ, as we abide daily in the light of His teachings, so that every word, thought, and act are in harmony with the whole, we become more and more conscious of the Oneness. It is then we are privileged to hear His voice and know the comfort of His abiding presence.

[11]John 10:30

Conclusion

Our God is a God of the physical, mental, and spiritual realms. Let us not lose sight of His activity in every plane and through every force. Our own desires and wills may sometimes blind us to the true requirements for adequate expression in any or all of these planes. We must constantly examine ourselves. In whatever plane of activity we may find ourselves, let us seek the most perfect expression of the God Force. Every atom of our physical bodies should vibrate in harmony. Our minds should be in constant touch with and filled with that which is stimulating and uplifting, guided and directed by a purpose to reach an ideal that is set in Him.

Let us not be discouraged; it is little by little, line upon line, that we grow in grace, in knowledge, and in the understanding of His ways. They are not hidden, nor far away, but are revealed to those who will hear and see the glory of the Oneness in the Father.

Let us examine ourselves to see how sincere is our desire to know that the Lord our God is One. Is it sufficient to be active rather than passive? If we would gain the concept, we must believe that He is, and that He rewards those who seek to do His will. He is life. We are to make our desires, our hearts, our minds, and our souls one with Him in bringing to the knowledge of all that the power of God, through the Christ, is able to cause us to know that "there is one God; and there is none other but He: and to love Him with all the heart, and with all the understanding, and with all the soul, and with all the strength, and to love his neighbor as himself, is more than all whole burnt offerings and sacrifices."[12]

> As my body, mind and soul are one, Thou, O Lord, in the manifestations in the earth, in power, in might, in glory, art one. May I see in that I do, day by day, more of that realization, and manifest the more.   *262-38*

[12]Mark 12:32-33

Lesson XII

LOVE

"And now abideth faith, hope, love, these three; but the greatest of these is love."   I Corinthians 13:13 [RV]

Affirmation

Our Father, through the love that Thou has manifested in the world through Thy Son, the Christ, make us more aware of "God is love."   *262-43*

XII

LOVE

[Based on Edgar Cayce readings 262-43 through 262-48]

Introduction

Love is God. The whole law is fulfilled in these three words. Humanity is urged to observe and to cultivate this attribute, for it is through love that physical life is perfected and the continuity of life realized. Life is Creative Force in action and is the expression of love.

Love, divine love, is universal. It is found in the smile of a babe, which indeed is love undefiled, in the beauty of a song, and in a soul raised in praise to the Giver of Light. There is love manifested in the performance of duty when there is no thought of personal gain, in speaking encouraging words to those seeking an understanding, and in the activities of those doing their best with the talents entrusted to them. Love may be found in a contented heart that is willing to wait until the time is fulfilled when the ideal may be realized. Love that passes understanding is found in His Consciousness.

Love Manifested

It is the privilege of every soul to find joy in communing with God in nature; for each creation is a complete unit of expression of the Creative Power.

Christ perfectly manifested the love of the Maker. His life and teachings are the inspiration for the regeneration of all humanity. As children of God we can manifest God's love if we allow Him to have His way in our lives. Joy comes through service even in toil and pain. Pure undefiled love is so powerful that all may lay down their lives for others. Self is forgotten.

123

Then, come ye, my children! Harken unto that which thou
hast attained in thine self, that ye may put on the whole armor
and be fruitful in the love of Him [who] calls that *everyone*
should hear, should know, should understand, that God is in
His heavens and that His love endureth even to those who
harden their hearts—and wills that no one should perish
rather that in the love as may be manifested in the daily walks,
the daily activities of every soul, each may show through that
manifested the love which impels the giving of everything
within self as a manifestation of He, the Master having spoken
with thee!   *262-44*

The Power of Love

Love is the force that uplifts and inspires humankind. Children
starve without it. Men and women wither and decay when it is
lacking. It costs nothing, yet its value cannot be measured by
material standards. It can lift wretched human beings from the
miry clay of despair and set their feet upon the solid rock of
respectability and service.

Love is that inexplicable force which brought Jesus to earth so
that through Him the way back to the Father might be made
plain to the children of men. It caused the Father to give His Son
that whosoever believes might have eternal life. Love is that
dynamic force which brings into manifestation all things. It is
the healing force, the cleansing force, and the force that blesses
all things we touch. With our hearts filled with love we will see
only goodness and purity in everybody and in everything. In the
beginning love looked upon the earth and saw that it was good
and blessed it.

As love is God, it is, therefore, our abundant supply. Do we
lack? Do we love? Do we allow conditions to keep us from the
realization of the presence of God? If so, how can we expect the
flow of abundance, when we are keeping the channel blocked by
our thoughts and attitudes? We are standing in the way of our
own success. When conditions arise which seem hard to endure,
if we would realize that we are workers together with God and
that each condition is perhaps some problem in our lives that
must be met and overcome, we might stop and count our blessings
instead of counting our hardships. Only with our hearts filled
with love—love for conditions, love for people, love for God—can

we fully realize this. Life is growth. We never can grow in knowledge and understanding and really be channels of blessings until we have endured and conquered in ourselves just the things that we would help others to overcome. Love allows no place for hate and recognizes no evil, but sees all things working together for good. The power of love is unlimited. We alone may set the metes and bounds. We may use it constructively or selfishly. We may uplift our fellow humans or crush ideals, instigate revolts, and wreck civilization. It all depends upon whether we are in love with ourselves or are willing to lay down our lives for others.

The Test of Love

"Love suffereth long, and is kind . . . beareth all things, believeth all things, hopeth all things, endureth all things."[1] Can we truthfully say, "I am persuaded, that neither death, nor life, nor angels, nor principalities, nor powers, nor things present, nor things to come, nor height, nor depth, nor any other creature, shall be able to separate us from the love of God, which is in Christ Jesus our Lord?"[2] The Master said, "This is my commandment, that ye love one another, as I have loved you."[3] "Greater love hath no man than this, that a man lay down his life for his friends."[4] "Love your enemies . . . that ye may be the children of your Father which is in heaven: for He maketh his sun to rise on the evil and on the good, and sendeth rain on the just and on the unjust."[5] They that do not love their worst enemy have not even begun to develop. The Father's love is the golden thread, that is woven throughout the Scriptures, which enlarges and spreads until the whole law is fulfilled in "God so loved the world, that he gave his only begotten Son, that whosoever believeth in him should not perish, but have everlasting life."[6] To fulfill the law of love is more than simply to love those who love us, for by so doing we have not reached the faintest conception of divine love.

Love is giving out the best that is within us. Then, where slights, slurs, or even suspicions have been allowed to affect us, love cannot mean all that it should in our experience. The Master asks of us that we love Him, that we keep His commandments that He may abide with us, even as He abides with the Father. All of us believe, all know, and all understand that those things

[1] I Cor. 13:4, 7 [RV]   [2] Romans 8:38-39   [3] P.R. See John 13:34
[4] John 15:13   [5] Matt. 5:44, 45   [6] John 3:16

that hinder are caused by selfishness. This prevents even the dawn of the concept of what love should mean to us. Few of us have found the love that makes us free indeed, that keeps us from making unkind remarks, and prevents us from being disappointed in things, in people, and in conditions. How much are we willing to bear, to do, and to suffer that others may become aware of the love of the Father?

Love Is Giving

The law of love does not do away with other laws, but makes the law of recompense, the law of faith, the law of earth forces of effect—not defective but effective. Love is that attribute of the soul that enables us to give, asking nothing in return. Christ exemplified this in His life, in His death, and in His parting promise after His resurrection, "Lo, I am with you alway, even to the end of the age."[7] If humanity could get the vision of what it means to love as He loves, what peace would come on earth!

Do we want the best for another before our own wants and desires are satisfied? Can we see some good in all whom we meet? This is the Christ way of showing love. Where we are weak, He is ready to sympathize, comfort, and supply strength. In His name there is power. If we call on His name, if we abide in His teachings, we will radiate such a glow of righteousness (right thinking and acting) that those who sit in darkness will see great light.

Let us take hold on things of the spirit, for they alone are eternal. "The children of Light are called even now into service that His day may be hastened, lest many faint."[8] Do we not remember our years and years of service for our families and for our friends, in which every act was so prompted by love that there was never a thought of being weary? When our best years have been spent for them and we are no longer needed or seemingly appreciated, does sadness fill our hearts? Let us not forget that such service is never lost, for with love it has been woven into the souls of those for whom we worked. It will shine forth again and again in the lives of many yet unborn. Love never dies; it is eternal.

[7]P.R. See Matt. 28:20   [8]P.R.

Divine Love Passes Understanding

Undoubtedly, the reason that humankind does not totally accept the way back to the Father, made perfect through the Christ, is that so great a love as the Father showed forth for His children passes understanding. God, the Father, the First Cause, in the manifestations of Self brought the world, as we observe it about us, into being through love. He gave to us, His creation, the ability to become one with Him. This way was shown through the Christ, the Mediator with the Father. Hence we realize that God so loved the world that He gave His only begotten Son, that we through Him might have life—God more abundant.

> ... "Ye that have known me knoweth my Father also, for I am in Him, and ye in me"—may know that love that maketh the life burn as an ember in a darkened and unregenerated world. "For unto me must come all that would find the way. I *am* the Way. Ye are my brethren. Ye have been begotten in the flesh through the love made manifest in the earth." Then, in the spirit and in the mind that hast brought thee to that understanding and consciousness of His love made manifest, abide ye day by day.   *262-44*

Personal Experiences

"I was seeking to know and experience that love that passes understanding. I soon found that if I would love I must know Him who is the Author of Love. The way was pointed out to me: Commune the more often in the inner shrine, in the Holy of Holies. Meet the presence of the Father there; know the love of the Christ in action; experience and see the power of the Holy Spirit."

"In meditation I found the peace that I had been seeking for months. It was not far away, but very near, even within my heart. I came to know that my Redeemer lives, that His presence may be experienced, and that my body, mind, and soul may be one with Him."

"In a trying experience I sought divine love. I realized more and more the consciousness of the presence of the Father and the consolation that I was being watched over by guardian angels. Peace filled my soul. 'Herein is love, not that we loved God, but that He loved us, and sent His Son to be the propitiation for our sins.' "[9]

[9]I John 4:10

"I have found that in sending out thoughts of love to any person or thing the whole environment may be changed. My child was very cross one night. She did not want to study or obey any of my requests. I began to look at her and send her thoughts of love. She seemed to get them very quickly, for in a short while her face was wreathed in smiles, and without further trouble she came to the table and began to study. Instantly, her whole attitude changed to one of obedience. Not a word was said; love alone conquered."

"The law that brought worlds into existence is the same law that makes us friends with all of God's creatures. My children were great lovers of pets and were ready to adopt any they found homeless or friendless. My experience deals with a homeless cat which made frequent visits to our back yard. She was so wild that she would run if she saw or heard anyone approach. We would leave food for her, but she was so filled with fear that she did not dare let us see her eat it.

"By our constant kindness in caring for her and showing our love, for we had come to love and pity her, she finally dropped her fear and would let us pet her, and if permitted would even come into the house. It took two years to accomplish this, but we succeeded. Truly, 'Love casteth out fear.' "[10]

The power of love may work in the lives of individuals in material ways as well as spiritual, as indicated in the following experience:

"Someone that I dearly loved was in need of financial help. One morning when it seemed I had on me all I could bear, from a material standpoint, he came to me and asked for a loan of a hundred dollars. I felt that he was asking for my all, as I had only a little more in the bank from which I could draw and did not know when I would be able to get more. It seemed as if I were a child and someone had asked for my last penny, which I wanted very much.

"In my dilemma, the thought came to me that I could not reject my friend, but should go to the bank and let him have it, for his mental distress outweighed my desire for self-preservation. There followed many constructive as well as conflicting thoughts. Should I take almost all I had and give to another? Was I called on to make such a sacrifice? Finally, there came to me a realization of the great sacrifice made for me, and the love of the Heavenly

[10]See I John 4:18

Father for His children. My conflicting thoughts vanished and I had peace. For had He not promised, 'I will never leave thee, nor forsake thee'?[11]

"The power of love is slowly molding the lives of us all. I know this because of its influence in helping me day by day to show forth His love and to live in the way that He may be glorified through my service to others."

Conclusion

Come ye, my children, in that ye have all been called unto that way which would show forth to thy neighbor, thy brethren, that the Father loved His children. Who *are* His children? They that keep His commandments day by day. For unto him that is faithful and true is given the crown of life. The harvest is ripe, the laborers are few. Be not weary because there has been that which has *seemed* to trouble thee, for the ways are being opened to those that show themselves faithful and true. Faint not, for the day of the Lord is near at hand. *262-47*

Our Father, through the love that Thou hast manifested in the world through Thy Son, the Christ, make us more aware of "God is love." *262-43*

GOD IS LOVE

"If I speak with the tongues of men and of angels, but have not love, I am become sounding brass, or a clanging cymbal. And if I have the gift of prophecy, and know all mysteries and all knowledge; and if I have all faith, so as to remove mountains, but have not love, I am nothing. And if I bestow all my goods to feed the poor, and if I give my body to be burned, but have not love, it profiteth me nothing. Love suffereth long, and is kind; love envieth not; love vaunteth not itself, is not puffed up, doth not behave itself unseemly, seeketh not its own, is not provoked, taketh not account of evil; rejoiceth not in unrighteousness, but rejoiceth with the truth; beareth all things, believeth all things, hopeth all things, endureth all things. Love never faileth: but whether there be prophecies, they shall be done away, whether there be tongues, they shall cease; whether there be knowledge, it shall be done away. For we know in part, and we prophesy in part: but when that which is perfect is come, that which is in part

[11]Hebrews 13:5

shall be done away. When I was a child, I spake as a child, I felt
as a child, I thought as a child: now that I am become a man, I
have put away childish things. For now we see in a mirror,
darkly; but then face to face: now I know in part; but then shall
I know even as also I have been known. But now abideth faith,
hope, love, these three; and the greatest of these is love."

I Corinthians 13 [RV]

A Search for God

BOOK II

Published by
A.R.E. Press
Virginia Beach, Virginia

Printed in U.S.A.

PREFACE

In the preface of *A Search for God,* Book I, we have the explanation for the compilation of these lessons.

It was stated that twelve individuals (more at the beginning of the study) dedicated themselves to the task of giving to others the basic principles of soul development that came through the psychic readings of Edgar Cayce.

This they could do only through prayer, meditation, and endeavoring to live each lesson. For they must know that such lessons were workable in their own lives and therefore would be in the lives of others.

The Way made perfect is seen in the man Jesus who became the Christ; and who, through the spiritualization of the physical body by overcoming the desires of the flesh, was able to resurrect the body.

> Hence, as there came the development of that first entity of flesh and blood through the earth plane, He became *indeed* the Son—through the things which He experienced in the varied planes, as the development came to the oneness with the position in that which man terms the Triune . . .
>
> In materiality we find some advance faster, some grow stronger, some become weaklings. Until there is redemption through the acceptance of the law (or love of God, as manifested through the Channel or the Way), there can be little or no development in a material or spiritual plane. But all must pass under the rod, even as He—who entered into materiality.
>
> *5749-3*

In this course of study the following excerpt will be helpful to those seeking deeper understanding:

> In giving that as might be significant in the experiences of [all], it is well that there be considered those conditions which

133

exist in the world of thought, as well as in the political and economic situations throughout the world—if there is to be a practical application of the significance of the resurrection of Jesus, the Christ.

The life, the death, the resurrection of Jesus are as facts, in the hearts and minds of those here. The resurrection of Jesus, the Christ, is a significant fact to each individual only according to how he applies same (as it is significant to him) in his daily life, experience and conversation with his fellow man.

Then, in a material world—a world of hate, of divided opinions—what is the course that you each will pursue, in relationships to your fellow men?

Is it the course outlined by the tenets, the principles which He, the Teacher of teachers, gave as respecting the manner of life, of activity, that you each would give in your dealings and relationships with your fellow men?

We know, and only need to be reminded, that the whole law is in Him. For, as He gave that which is the basis, the principle, of the intent and desire and purpose which should prompt our activity, so we in our own world—as we live, as we speak, as we pray—are to let it be in that tempo, in that way and manner which was prompted by Him, as He taught His disciples how to pray.

Then as we analyze this prayer in our experience, we see what the life, the death, the resurrection of Jesus the Christ—who is the way, the truth, the light—must mean in this period in the experience of man.

Think not that He, God, will be mocked. For whatsoever a man soweth, that must he also reap. This was truly exemplified in the life of the Man of Galilee. For in Him we all live, we all move, we all die. So, in Him we are all made alive.

Then put away hate, malice, jealousy, or the taking sides with any that stir up strife.

Be ye rather on the Lord's side, knowing that no man is in any position of power or might save by the will of the Father, that there may be fulfilled that which has been promised of Him, by Him and through that advent of the man Jesus into a material world.

Then, as ye meditate upon the meaning of the resurrection of this man of God, know that the way is open to thee to approach the throne of God; not as an excuse, not as a justification, but rather in love, in harmony, in that which brings hope for a sin-sick world.

Each individual, then, may act, may live, may pray —in his or her own little sphere of activity—in such a manner as to bring peace and harmony, even among those who APPEAR to be at variance to the cause of the Christ in the material world.

Let not thy heart be troubled, then. Ye believe in God; believe also in Him—who came to bring peace, and the way to the Father, exemplifying same in the ability to take away death— that is as sin in the experience of man.

And thus may he (man) indeed love the Lord with all his heart, and his neighbor as himself.   *5749-12*

Lesson I

OPPORTUNITY

Affirmation*

In seeking to magnify Thy Name, Thy Glory, through that
Thou dost make manifest in me, O Lord, be Thou the Guide,
and—day by day, as the opportunity is given—let my hands, my
mind, my body, do that Thou wouldst have me do as Thine own
in the earth; for, as I manifest, may Thy glory become known to
those through the love, the promises Thou hast made in Thy Son.

262-49

*Before starting *A Search for God*, Book II, it is suggested that the "Meditation"
chapter on page 1 be reviewed by the group.

I

OPPORTUNITY

[Based on Edgar Cayce readings 262-49 through 262-54]

Definition

Opportunity is a material manifestation of a spiritual ideal. Through a physical body the soul has an opportunity to express the attainments developed in other spheres of consciousness. Life in the earth becomes an opportunity for paralleling, correlating, cooperating, bringing into existence the effects of using all experience presented for the development of the soul. Hence, opportunity, primarily, is material manifestation of spiritual actions in conscious forces of the material plane. (See 262-50.)

Opportunities Come Through Cooperation

Cooperation is making ourselves a channel of blessings to others. Each day, each hour, in fact, each thought, provides an opportunity for "giving." What can we give? Peter said, "Silver and gold have I none; but *such as I have* give I thee: In the name of Jesus Christ of Nazareth rise up and walk."[1]

Each one of us is in a *particular* job, a *particular* home, a *particular* city, state, and nation because we have prepared ourselves for this pattern. It is a time and place of our choice. We must begin our service here, now. A smile, a kind word, a healing thought, these we have and can give. For the life of self bespeaks the thoughts of the heart; and each shall so live that He, the Christ, becomes the opportunity for all who meet thee—whether at the table, in sleep, or walking in the street. (See 262-50.)

The Master went about doing good, making every opportunity a material manifestation of His spiritual ideal. Those who follow

[1]Acts 3:6

His example have placed upon themselves no great burden, for they have comfort in His words, "Inasmuch as ye have done it unto one of the least of these my brethren, ye have done it unto me."[2]

Thus, cooperation must be put into the pattern of our daily lives. Through simple thoughts and acts we prepare for the greater opportunities that lie ahead of each soul.

A Knowledge of Self Helps Us to Recognize More Opportunities

Spiritual forces have so long been considered as being in the misty realm of theory that we are, as children, just becoming aware that our soul faculties can be applied in everyday life, and that this awakening within makes us more useful in a material world. Therefore, being more conscious of our opportunities is a result of the awakening of our inner spiritual faculties—our entering into a new world, the world of spiritual youth. As we develop, there will come urges and aptitudes previously unknown. Calls to service will come. May we be ready and willing.

Each trial met and overcome is a means toward development. We should realize that each experience is an opportunity to test, to train, and to strengthen us. It is only little by little that we are able to overcome all things.

> In seeking to know that opportunity that is given each in the present, it is one thing to live that there may be presented to another that which will open another's opportunity; and it is for *self* to recognize and use the opportunity in self's own development.   *262-50*
>
> *Do* ever in self that thou knowest to be right, though it may make of self even an outcast to thine neighbor.   *373-2*

If we do not watch ourselves and know that of ourselves we can do nothing, our life may become clogged with egotism, bitter resentment, petty jealousies, and evil thinking. We may fall so low that we can scarcely see good in any condition, person or thing. We should know self well enough to realize that the fault is within us, and that we have within just what we see in others, else how could we recognize it? We must open the door to our inner selves and let in the Christ light, let our wills be one with His, listen to His voice, heed His call. To know self is an

[2]Matt. 25:40

opportunity. To know self to be one with God is the supreme opportunity of man.

The Higher the Ideal, the Greater Are the Opportunities

Each and every soul must come to the consciousness of being a service in the activities of that it, the soul, worships in the infinite sphere or spiritual force. *262-50*

Christ, who is the Way, the Truth, and the Light, is the highest ideal. By holding to any lesser ideal for thought and action we build a fence around ourselves; we confine ourselves to conventionalities; we block the gate to service.

We must be free—free to think our own thoughts, free to live our own lives—and this freedom must be born of an attunement with an unlimited idea. "Know the truth and the truth shall make you free."[3] What is Truth?

Remember, "If ye abide in me, and my words abide in you, ye shall ask what ye will, and it shall be done unto you. Herein is my Father glorified that ye bear much fruit; so shall ye be my disciples."[4] "Without me ye can do nothing."[5] Without Christ, we could not of ourselves even recognize our opportunities, so filled would we be with self and selfish interests.

Let the meditations of the heart, let those activities of the body, bespeak that thou wouldst offer in self as an opportunity or channel for another to seek, to know, thy God. *262-50*

Faith Helps Us Grasp Opportunity

An opportunity to demonstrate spiritual truth may come our way. Our so-called better judgment, from the material standpoint, may suggest that it is wiser to step aside and let it pass; for if there is to be a failure, it would be better for another to have the experience rather than have it ourselves. There is lack of faith in such reasoning. Faith is the inner spiritual knowledge of the Creative Forces of the Universe. It cannot be recognized by others who do not have the same inner guidance. They may call it poor judgment.

With faith we can move mountains of doubt, prove that thoughts are things and that words have power. Physical, mental, and spiritual demonstrations take place when no way seems open.

[3]John 8:32 [4]John 15:7-8 [5]John 15:5

Using what we have in hand, doing with all our might what our hands find to do, let us seize each opportunity. It is ours to act, to plan, to work; it is for Him, the author of faith, to give the increase. We may profess to have faith; but it is our actions that show how much we believe. As we study, as we meditate, as we seek to use each opportunity, our faith in Christ, in the Father, in our neighbor, in ourselves, will grow. He has promised that help, strength, and understanding sufficient for all our needs will be supplied.

There will come tests—in the physical, the mental, the spiritual life. At these times we should rely on His promise, "I will never leave thee, nor forsake thee."[6] Are we to be carried about by every wind of doctrine? Shall we fear as those who have no hope? In the trials and tests through which the world is passing, where are we found? Are we stepping out on faith, knowing that His presence is with us? Are we giving hope, faith, and comfort to those who have not had our opportunities? Do we not feel that we are called at this time to let our light shine in the dark places of doubt and fear? Is our faith firm in what has been promised, and are we passing it on to others? If not, we are weaklings who are drifting, and falling short of the calling whereunto we have been called. "Watch ye, stand fast in the faith, quit you like men, be strong."[7] "For the day of the Lord is at hand."[8]

Opportunities Found in Fellowship

What opportunity does fellowship with the Father offer? Surely we have experienced the relief that comes when we go to Him with our sorrows. It is there that our problems are solved, there that we find the peace that passes understanding.

The acknowledgment of our physical weaknesses becomes an opportunity for exercising our greater strength—the Divine within. As we take advantage of an opportunity in one direction, the Divine within helps us to recognize others. We know that we have fellowship with the Father if we love others and seek to serve them. Everywhere there are such opportunities, so we should be on our guard, to be sure that we use wisdom and discretion, to be sure that we recognize the opportunities that will take us onward toward the supreme opportunity, which is to be one with Him in desire and purpose. What is the Way? As He

[6]Heb. 13:5   [7]I Cor. 16:13   [8]Joel 1:15

has given to those to whom He spoke, to whom He will speak, "... lovest thou me more than these? ... feed my lambs ... lovest thou me? ... feed my sheep."[9]

[Symbolically] the sheep represent those that know of, and know, the Way. The lambs represent those that seek, that would know, that would find the Way, that would come if shown the tenderness expressed in "The good shepherd feedeth the sheep; he tendeth the lambs." 262-51

We must both feed the sheep and tend the lambs.

Opportunities Are Recognized Through Virtue and Understanding

With virtue comes understanding and with understanding comes all the power and privilege of Divine Light. Armed with the weapons of spiritual warfare, we are able to enlarge our fields of helpfulness. We can, as with a two-edged sword, divide the right from the wrong, the true from the false, and be able to attempt greater things in His Name.

Life in the earth is a manifestation of God. It is no wonder, then, that we love to think of it as everlasting. Yet, when we misuse our opportunities, we misapply the knowledge we have of life and reap the results. If we do good, good must return to us, for "like begets like," not as a reward, but as a result of law. The result is spiritual understanding, which is a growth in spiritual development.

The direction in which we turn the activities of our life depends upon how we think, for "As he thinketh in his heart, so is he."[10] All power, all force, all life is from one source; if we misuse any portion of it, either by thought or action, we do not destroy it for it is of God, but we darken our own way; we dim the light that might be a help to others.

Many are wise in their own conceit; and often, as the Master said, "the children of this world are in their generation wiser than the children of light,"[11] since they use what light they have, even though they use it selfishly.

On such a basis the Athenians built an altar to the Unknown God. Paul declared that they ignorantly worshiped this Unknown God. For such a message he would have had to forfeit his life, if

---

[9]John 21:15, 16   [10]Proverbs 23:7   [11]Luke 16:8

he had not clothed it in wisdom and delivered it with understanding. He knew the Athenian law against the introduction of other gods, so he took them where they were and preached God, the Father, "in him we live, and move, and have our being,"[12] whom, he said, "ye ignorantly worship."[13] In the same manner we must watch our opportunities. We must be in such close touch with the infinite source of understanding that we at all times may render the right service in the right place.

Our Opportunities Should Be Met in Patience

In exercising patience we learn to recognize daily the little opportunities which are so important. Impatience to do great things blinds us. We should count it a privilege to be a servant of the servants in the Kingdom of God. Our servant is God's free individual; for in service to humanity we are making our wills one with His.

To do this requires patience with ourselves as well as with others. "In your patience possess ye your souls."[14] It is possible to have a thing and yet not possess it. Our soul has within it all the attributes of the Divine. It is worth waiting, striving, working to understand and know ourselves to be individual and yet one with God. Let us not be in haste, but count each step as an opportunity.

The Open Door Is the Way into
Greater Fields of Opportunity

Faint not in well doing, for there is being opened the door for greater opportunities.   *262-51*

Perception of truth is a growth in consciousness. Our finite minds cannot grasp all truth; however, doors are continually being opened through which we may go to greater concepts of truth, to greater understanding of the boundless love of the Father. There is being opened glory in the Spirit of Truth that convinces us of the knowledge of our relationship with the Father.

Now, as never before, there is open a door that none can close; for His word must be fulfilled, ". . . they shall all know me, from the least of them unto the greatest."[15]

---

[12]Acts 17:28   [13]Acts 17:23   [14]Luke 21:19   [15]Jer. 31:34

It Is an Opportunity to Realize His Presence

When we seek to keep His Presence as a thing apart, something to be experienced, something to be aware of when we are disturbed in some manner, we lose sight of the fact that to abide in His Presence is the experience, the knowledge, the understanding, the opportunity of all as we seek to do His biddings. His Presence abides with us always, for it is in Him that we live and move and have our being. We must recognize this, come to know and understand it, to realize that we are children of the Most High. To be aware of His Presence is our heritage, our great opportunity in this material plane.

Opportunities Found in the Cross, in the Crown

Have we had a cross to bear lately? If we counted it an opportunity, it was easier to carry. Maybe we learned just the lesson we most needed in this experience. Know in whom thou hast believed, for the spirit of Right guards those who choose His way in directing the mental and spiritual life; "And know that all things work together for good to them that love God . . ."[16] May we bear each cross with such a spirit and feel that all things are working together for our good.

This was exemplified in Him who is the Master of masters. It is a great opportunity to live day by day in such a manner that the Christ spirit may shine within, to heal and to bless.

The Opportunity to Know That the Lord Thy God Is One

When the divinity of Jesus was declared by Peter, Jesus said to him, "Blessed art thou, Simon Bar-jona: for flesh and blood hath not revealed it unto thee, but my Father which is in heaven."[17] Just so, to realize the oneness of all force—the Lord thy God is one—is an opportunity that comes through divine inspiration.

In order to have this experience we must conform to the things of spirit. Peter forsook all and followed the Master. Do we? That is not easy to do when viewed from a worldy standpoint; but if we pay the price, we too may see the glory of the oneness made perfect in Him.

There should be gladness in our activities. We should be on fire

[16]Romans 8:28   [17]Matt. 16:17

to use every opportunity to show that we realize that, "Hear, O Israel: the Lord our God is one Lord."[18] Are our wills one with His, or are they seeking to glorify our own desires, our own selfish interests? We should know that the way is not long, nor is the cross more grievous than we can bear, if our trust is in Him.

It Is an Opportunity to Love

We can recognize now as never before those attributes of the soul, that are ours to be used. Gradually, we come to realize the Presence of the Father, the oneness of all force, and the fact that the way back to perfection is through Him who is the Way, the Truth and the Life. This is made perfect in love. To love is the noblest expression of humankind. It is not simply of God, it is God; and as we manifest it, we manifest the God force that is within us. Whether in the physical, mental, or spiritual body, this power is the strongest and most dominant influence.

To love is our greatest opportunity. It brings happiness as nothing else does. All that is good is made a part of us as we seek to express love for our fellow human beings. Thoughts, words, acts, are opportunities for us to express this force day by day.

> Consecrate yourselves, your bodies, your minds, your abilities in *every* direction, to the opportunities to be of service to those ye meet and contact day by day.   262-53

As we may ignorantly destroy a priceless painting with a few scratches, so may we, in misusing and misdirecting our forces, mar our bodies, our minds, our souls, in such a way that only a God of Love can recognize us. Though we may direct love into many channels, there is only One through whom there will be a realization of love made perfect, and that is found in Him, who said, "A new commandment I give unto you, that ye love one another."[19]

The time draws near, the time is at hand, when there is more and more seeking for light and understanding. Let us then, in His way, manifest from day to day the love that has been showered upon us. May we so live that our lives become an example to those who seek.

May we pray:

> The Lord guide Thou [me] Thy servant in the ways [that he] should go.

[18]Deut. 6:4   [19]John 13:34

"Let my going in, mine coming out, be wholly within the ways
Thou would have me go. Direct my steps, direct my mind. Let
Thy will be done in me; for, as the heart panteth after Thy own
will, may my spirit bear witness—in the things my body does
day by day—that the Lord is in His Holy Temple, and the rod
has not passed from those that call on His name. For the *glory*
of the Father to the sons of men may be expressed in those that
would guide, guard and keep the holy ways."   *262-51*

A Pictorial Sketch of
A Search for God

" That the purpose be for real study and increase in knowledge. "

Above: *A transcription of the first session in which the sleeping Edgar Cayce began the* Search for God *psychic readings on September 14, 1931.*

The material that inspired the *Search for God* books came through the sleeping Edgar Cayce in special sessions delivered on Sunday afternoons from 1931 through 1942.

Presented in the form of "lessons," the information had to be lived by group members before the next lesson would be given.

In 1934 Mr. Cayce told the group members that the *Search for God* lessons would still be studied 100 years later.

Right: *Edgar Cayce as he appeared during the 1930s*

Conducted by Edgar Cayce's wife Gertrude, the readings that paved the way for *A Search for God* were given at the homes of various group members.

On Monday evenings, the group would meet in order to discuss the material that was received the previous day. Their discussions became the main body of the *Search for God* texts.

Left: *Edgar and Gertrude Cayce, 1935*

As with all of Cayce's psychic readings, secretary Gladys Davis (later Turner) stenographically recorded then transcribed the readings that inspired the *Search for God* lessons.

Right: *Gladys Davis, 1928*

Hugh Lynn Cayce, Edgar's son, was present at the first study group meeting in the home of Florence and Edith Edmonds. He attended the meetings throughout the study group years until he was called to serve in WWII in April of 1943.

Right: *Hugh Lynn Cayce, 1932*

It was Florence Edmonds who first suggested to Edgar Cayce that a group be started to study the information in his psychic readings.

Left: *A young Florence Edmonds, early 1920s*

Above: *Edith Edmonds'
question to Edgar Cayce,
written in August of 1931,
asks, "In what way could
we as a group best serve
God, our fellow man, and
assist in the development
of the Association for
Research and Enlight-
enment, Inc.?"*

*This question, among
others, brought forth the
first responses from Cayce
which would form the
Search for God lessons.*

Left: *Edith Edmonds,
1930*

2/14/66 GD's note: Tonight at Group #1 meeting Noah Miller
gave me these minutes which Hannah Miller kept from 4/27/31 through
8/29/32. Notice that minutes 4/27/31 through 5/21/31 preceded the
readings for the group in the 262 series.

On the evening of April 27ᵗʰ 1931, an interested groups met at the Home of the Misses Edmonds to discuss ways and means of starting a study club group. Mr. Hugh Lynn Cayce acted as leader. After many exchanges of ideas from the different individuals the following was decided upon.

That we meet every Monday night at the home of one of the group.

That for the month of May we study Comparative Religions. The text book being "This Believing World" by Lewis Browne, together with helps from other distinguished writers.

That the purpose be for real study and increase in knowledge.

The group also decided to pay the expenses attached to the lecture to be given by Mr. Edgar Cayce at The Monticello Hotel on Tuesday Evening Apr. 27ᵗʰ The Amt. being $10.00. There being fourteen present each promised to pay 75 cts. That has been paid.

Miss Esther Wynne was elected Chairman.
Mrs. Hannah C. Miller. Secretary.
Closed 10:30 P.M. Meet with Mrs. Black on May 4ᵗʰ.
H. C. Miller. Secr.

Above: *Hannah Miller's minutes of the first meeting of "an interested group," April 27, 1931.*

Left: *Hannah Miller, 1950*

Before they had a name, members of the first study group called themselves the "Study Club." They eventually came to be known as Norfolk Study Group #1. The work of that first group has given birth to over 1,200 *A Search for God* study groups world-wide.

Above: *Standing, l. to r.: Esther Wynne, Gladys Davis, Fannie Freeman, Helen Storey, Florence Edmonds, Helen Ellington, L.B. Cayce, Mildred Davis, Mary Louise Black, Hugh Lynn Cayce, Edith Edmonds, Hannah Miller, Frances Y. Morrow. Sitting, l. to r.: C.A. Barrett, C.W. Rosborough, Jeanne LeNoir and her mother Ruth LeNoir in back, Eloise Potter, Minnie Barrett, Gertrude Cayce, and Leona Rosborough.*

Photo taken by Edgar Cayce, April 17, 1932

About Study Group Membership

I am a relatively new student of the Search for God *material. My study group began a repeat of Book I last May, since there were several new members in the group. As the months have gone by, and we have studied and applied the lessons, I have found my life enriched in ways I never could have anticipated. To me, the* Search for God *lessons have become a true "study course" in skills for living. My attitudes about my job, my family, my self, even my "enemies" are slowly (but surely) coming into greater attunement with the Creative Forces, and I find myself more content than I have ever been.* **R.F.**
1-year group member

I have gained immense pleasure as well as spiritual growth from the study group program these past few years and the continued use of the Search for God *books.*
The lessons always seem new to me, they are ever-applying for my ever-changing life. They help me realize my part in every situation that confronts me, and this can be a very humbling reality. The lessons continue to help me to "keep on keeping on." **B.B.**
3-year group member

Over the last twenty years two experiences—more than any others—have totally transformed my life. The first was coming in contact with the Edgar Cayce material and the second was becoming a part of A Search for God.
My study group changed my life. These ten people, coming together weekly to discuss everything from universal laws to personal relationships, impacted me (and my life) in ways that they may never know. The study group became my island in the sea of life. Regardless of what stressors I had at work, at home, or simply in my mind, my group was there for me. The funny thing was, we were exactly like a family—we didn't always get along or see eye to eye, but we always cared for one another. And in the caring and in the application of the material, real "magic" started to happen.
Although my job eventually moved me away from these people, my study group is (and always will be) a part of my life **K.T.**
4 1/2-year group member

The Edgar Cayce readings have brought me the beautiful message of life and a better relationship with my Creator; through them my heart sings. My study group—through its acceptance, its teachings, and its commitment—has made that song in my heart an everlasting melody. **D.B.**
23-year group member

I joined a Search for God *group . . . and it was a relief to find people I could talk to. As we went through Book I, I found my life changing. My group went slowly and we tried to live what we were learning.* **H.D.**
14-year group member

About Study Group Membership

I have been working with the Search for God *material for over thirty-five years. I have attended study groups in California, North Carolina, Texas, and Virginia. I get more excited the more I use the information.*

Over the years we have varied the way we use the material. When we started out, we would spend several months studying, discussing, and working with the affirmation and disciplines related to each chapter. Much later we took the discipline of doing one chapter a month and could really see and feel the growth within ourselves much more. Several times we have been through the original readings. At times we have set ourselves the discipline of reading in one month all the readings related to a topic. Right now we study one chapter the first meeting in each month, go over the affirmation so that we can use it daily, and then for the other weeks in the month study supplemental Cayce readings.

I love the Search for God *material. I know it to be life-transforming when studied and applied, and when the affirmation is used in daily meditation. There is a sequence of application that leads to the natural unfoldment of the soul. My study group is as enthusiastic as I am about the* Search for God *books.*

                                    M.A.P.
                                    36-year group member

I felt a strong inner prompting to find out about study groups in my area. I needed personal contact with like-minded people to develop and grow. My first meeting indicated to me the wonderful flow of life.

Besides offering me a great learning and sharing experience, the study group has helped me stay focused and centered. I have barely gotten my feet wet, yet I have already felt more growth and harmony in my life. I know that by continuing with my study group my learning will increase, my life will be enriched, and I will be challenging myself to be all that I can be.

                                    S.I.
                                    New group member

The study group material energizes my spiritual centers in an emotional and loving manner. As members work and seek together, we create a new pattern of mental and spiritual energy which transcends individual contributions and adds to the Light in the world. The group is a learning tool, a spiritual workshop. By assisting each other in prayer and meditation, we find (like the parable of the loaves and fishes) that our energy is multiplied tenfold.   B.R.
                                    12-year group member

Cayce's emphasis on the ideal has become the flagpole of a lifetime, from which my flag of purpose and spiritual service flies. Using the principle of "You are always seeing yourself in others," I have made immense changes in my workplace, relationships, and career. A sense of my worthiness as a creation of God and my role as a co-creator with God took form and substance in the group.

There are times when I questioned the wisdom of creating a life script that included study groups . . . and other times when I have been on my knees in gratitude to be a part of the group.

                                    D.S.
                                    4-year group member

Above: *Edith Edmonds' letter to Edgar Cayce asked if he would meditate with the study group. The formation of the Glad Helpers prayer group followed as a direct result of the work of Study Group #1.*

Norfolk, Va.
December 15, 1931

Dear Mr. Cayce:

We, the Glad group, want to radiate gladness everywhere, so we are sending a full measure, pressed down and running over to the one whom we have all learned to love and know.

We, as a group, want to thank you for your invaluable service rendered to us and want to cooperate with you in any way that we possibly can.

We would like for you to wholeheartedly enter into the spirit of meditation with us, meditating at 6:30 a.m.-7:00 a.m. and again at 6:00 p.m. Knowing that if we ask anything in His name, it will be done.

And may God's richest blessings be upon you and your household, and give you perfect peace that He alone can give.

Hoping to see you all real soon,

I am,
Sincerely yours,

Edith Mildred Edmonds

Above: *The first Glad Helpers prayer group formed in 1932: (l. to r.): Fannie Freeman, Florence Edmonds, Hugh Lynn Cayce, Mildred Davis, Edith Edmonds, Edgar Cayce, and Minnie Barrett.*

Norfolk Study Group #1 members came and went throughout the 1930s. Eventually, the remaining members of the original study group decided to limit its number to twelve.

Right: *These are the signatures of those who comprised the group at the time of the publication of* A Search for God, *Book I.*

Gertrude E. Cayce
Ruth D. LeNoir
Esther Wynne
Florence R. Edmonds
Frances Y. Morrow
Gladys Davis
Hugh Lynn Cayce
Hannah C. Miller
Helen Ellington
Noah L. Miller
Helen W. Storey.

Edgar Cayce

June 1942

Edgar Cayce himself asked Ruth LeNoir to join the A.R.E. in 1931, yet she was considered a "newcomer" when she joined the Norfolk Study Group in 1932. She remained with the group throughout the years when *A Search for God* was compiled.

Left: *Ruth LeNoir, early 1920s*

Frances Y. Morrow was the first official secretary of Norfolk Study Group #1. The lessons were distributed to members of other study groups, one at a time, throughout the 1930s, before they were finally assembled in book form in 1942.

Right: *Frances Y. Morrow, 1931*

Esther Wynne played the role of "compiler" of the manuscript, but she was also responsible for getting the first edition of Book I printed by William Byrd Press, Richmond, Virginia.

Right: *Esther Wynne, 1942*

Below: *Esther's note from April 20, 1938, discussing the preface to the lesson entitled "Spirit":*
"What is to be stressed in the preface of the book? That the intent is not to furnish informative data, but rather to give that which if lived, or as it is lived, in the experience of the individual, will answer to that within self for the assurance of not only soul awakening, soul developments, but the continuity of life."

February 3rd, 1942

The William Byrd Press, Inc.,
8 North 6th Street,
Richmond, Va.

Att: Mr. Richmond Maury, President

Gentlemen:

Your letter of January 21, addressed to Miss Esther Wynne
has been turned over to me.

We would like for you to proceed with the production of
the book, "A Search For God," copy for which, exclusive of
the Introduction, is in your hands.

Enclosed you will find our check for two hundred dollars
($200.00), covering approximately one third of the price
quoted us for one thousand copies. We agree to pay another
two hundred ($200.00), with the return of page proof and the
balance upon delivery.

It may be that we will desire another five hundred copies of
this book printed at the same time. Am I correct in assuming
that we may make a final decision on this when we return the
page proof?

What will be the approximate length of time required for the
production of this book?

We will send you the material for the Introduction within
a few days, together with the lettering which is to appear
on the cover. Do I understand correctly that you will
then suggest an arrangement of this lettering and advise us
of the exact cost of the dies?

I was sorry not to have seen you in Richmond, Mr. Maury,
when I stopped in your office a couple of weeks ago.

Thank you for your promptness and courtesy.

Sincerely yours,

Hugh Lynn Cayce
Manager

Above: *Hugh Lynn Cayce's letter of
February 3, 1942, officially authorized
the first printing of* A Search for God
*fourteen months before he was called to
serve during WWII.*

Above: *An excerpt from a letter of endorsement for the* Search for God *lessons
from Reverend Joseph B. Clower, Jr., pastor of First Presbyterian Church of
Virginia Beach, Va., in 1943.*

Hugh Lynn Cayce was 24 years old when his father began giving the readings
that inspired *A Search for God.*

After World War II, he worked with Esther Wynne in bringing *A Search for
God,* Book II, into print. The second volume wasn't published until 1950, even
though the readings had been given from 1931 through 1942.

Below: *Esther Wynne and Hugh Lynn Cayce, 1950*

About Study Group Membership

I am 28 years old. Before I was informed of Edgar Cayce and his readings, my beliefs were very rigid, and I lived a life of guilt and fear. My spiritual journey was in confusion between what was right or wrong even in choosing a religious group, since all groups seemed in conflict with each other.

In this confusion I cried to God for help and almost immediately He sent into my life a dear friend who introduced me to the ideas in the Cayce readings. I have since joined a study group and am no longer confused, but freed. I have found the difference being, before I worshiped God in fear, and now I worship Him in love.   L.C.
3-year group member

The study group has been my spiritual family traveling together on a special path. The most important part of the meetings has been the group meditations, plus the reminder of my ideals, my path, my purpose—to keep on track and in focus.

When I was new to study group work, someone told me it would help make me a better person. I hope that is true . . .
C.S.
18-year group member

We have read the Search for God *books in our study group, and I have truly found them to be a light in my life. I find the thoughts and the words to be comforting and enlightening. When I feel that I am not living up to my expectations, I need only to read a chapter or two to find hope and patience.*
L.S.
5-year group member

For me, the weekly gathering of our Search for God *study group is a conscious, prayerful happening, sharing God's love with one another and with the universe. An atmosphere of acceptance and sensitivity provides a setting in which the deepest experiences can be safely shared. Relating and interpreting our dream life is as important as understanding the daily application of lessons we are learning.*

With a fullness of His spirit, I am prepared to better meet daily challenges or opportunities with a greater sense of being centered, balanced, and protected. Our mission is clear—that the love of God be made manifest in our world. Although the forms may differ—such as with steam, water, or ice—the content is the same . . .
M.M.
8-year group member

I first encountered the Search for God *material in 1977. This event followed ten years of reading the popular books on Cayce that had presented extracts from the readings around particular themes.*

The Search for God *books were different, and I could tell immediately that they were a rare find. As I read the books, I could feel a holy presence settle around me—a spirit of peace, love, and hope.*

Needless to say, I read the books from cover to cover. Then I reread them. During my daily routine, I found myself pondering the ideas that this material quietly presented. I began relating to people and situations in new and creative ways. I discovered that these books contained transformative power. I consider A Search for God *a priceless, personal gift.*
C.F.
10 1/2- year group member

Above: *Helen Ellington, late 1920s*

Helen Ellington was the last surviving
member of the original *A Search for
God* study group. She passed over on
May 19, 1991, at the age of 101, after
a 70-year association with the A.R.E.

Right: *Helen Ellington, in 1984*

Lesson II

DAY AND NIGHT

Affirmation

In Thy mercies, O Heavenly Father,
 Wilt Thou be the guide
In the study of the manifestations
 Of Thy love, even as in
"Day unto day uttereth speech and
 Night unto night sheweth knowledge."
So may the activities of my life,
 As a representative of Thy love,
Be a manifestation in the earth.

262-54

II

DAY AND NIGHT

[Based on Edgar Cayce readings 262-54 through 262-57]

Introduction

Day and night are relative in relation to the earth. Viewed from an outer sphere, there would be only different shades of light and darkness as the earth moves about the sun. Conditions that exist in the material plane are but shadows of truth in the mental and spiritual planes.

". . . and God divided the light from the darkness. And God called the light day, and the darkness he called night."[1] Thus day and night are figures of speech, spiritual symbols of good and evil. Day is facing towards the source of light, which, to those who seek to do His biddings, is the Voice, the Word, the Life, the Light, that comes into the hearts, minds, souls of all to awaken them to their relationship to the source of Light. Night is facing away from the source of Light.

In the mental, *night* is the knowledge that the soul is out of harmony with God; day is the first period of awareness of a way back to the source of all power.

In a *figurative* sense, day and night represent periods of growth and of recuperation—in the earth, the activities of a day and a night of rest.

Why the Creation of the World?

All souls were created in the beginning. This beginning refers not to the earth, but the universe. "Let us make man in our image . . ."[2] is a description of a spiritual creation, for God is Spirit. ". . . and there was not a man to till the ground . . . And the Lord God formed man of the dust of the ground, and breathed

[1]Gen. 1:4-5   [2]Gen. 1:26

151

into his nostrils the breath of life; and man became a living soul."[3]
This was the second creation.

> ... all souls in the beginning were one with the Father. The
> separation or turning away brought evil. Then there became
> the necessity of the awareness of self's being out of accord with
> or out of the realm of blessedness ... By becoming aware in a
> material world *is*—or was—the only manner or way through
> which spiritual forces might become aware of their separation
> from the spiritual atmosphere, the spiritual surroundings, of
> the Maker.   *262-56*

So in passing through our various experiences, even as He, the
first Adam, our soul becomes aware of its separation from its
Creator. As the nature of our relationship to our Maker grows
clearer, we begin to walk more and more in the Light in our
physical experiences. We came here for this purpose.

Through experience, through suffering, we come to know day
and night, light and darkness, good and evil, even as the Son, the
Adam. "Though he were a Son, yet learned he obedience by the
things which He suffered."[4] Finally, we recognize that we are on
our way back to our source. This alone brings satisfaction to our
souls.

Day unto Day Uttereth Speech

Today is the day of opportunity. Each span of life is just
another extended opportunity for light to break forth within us.
We are enjoined to use that which we have in hand, and are then
promised that our needs for further development will be supplied.
A God of love waits for the awakening of each soul.

A majority of us devote the activities of a day to supplying
ourselves and others with the material things of earth. Bread,
shelter, clothing must be provided in proportion to the life
pattern which we have builded. These things and the luxuries
which seem necessary for the body's welfare cannot be made the
ideals motivating our daily activities. "But seek ye first the
kingdom of God, and His righteousness; and all these things
shall be added unto you."[5] What things? That which we need for
peace and contentment. That which we need for spiritual growth.
These will be added as we fill our days with activities motivated
by Truth, Life and Light.

[3]Gen. 2:5, 7   [4]Heb. 5:8   [5]Matt. 6:33

Would we have Light? Then turn within. Let us find the answer to the problem that is keeping us in the dark. Let us judge no one, not even self, but study to know how we are using the knowledge, the understanding, and the opportunities that have been given us.

> For, each individual must so live each day that he may look into the face of that he has spoken, that he has lived, and say: "By this I stand to be judged before myself, before my God."
>
> *257-123*

It is well that we take stock of ourselves to see if we are advancing or retarding our own growth. Are all our plans in keeping with that He would guide us to do, or in keeping with our own desires? Do we love material things of the world more than the praise of God? Then know that in the way we go is the means for a better understanding or a serious retardment. Remember, the mental is the builder, the spiritual is the guide or the life, the conditions built in material things are the results. While there may come the pleasures of those things of the world for the season, the step by step should be for each of us, "I show, in my relations to my fellow man, in my conversation, and in my deed, that which I consider to be the relationship to my Maker." (See 257-123.)

Let us face the question. Do material possessions prevent spiritual growth? The answer must be determined by each individual for himself or herself. An examination of attitudes about material things, a critical study of personal ideals relating to possessions, will provide the solution. Greed and selfishness over a loaf of bread can be as damaging as pride and avarice over great wealth. There must come to every soul the experience of both great poverty and great wealth. In eternity there is plenty of what we call time for both.

When we pass out of the body from the activities in material things, what carries on? Is it not that which we have built within ourselves through constructive or destructive forces? Then, if our activity is as boundless as eternity, let our steps be in the way of Light, that these may bring, not only to us, but to those who follow after, those things that make for better understanding of what life is. Let us study to show ourselves approved unto our Maker, and not be confused, nor consider that the spiritual or mental life is different from the material, but know that one is the reflection of the other. If we live in the Light, the shadows fall behind. If our face is turned from the Light, there can be nothing in life, in mental and material things, except shadows.

"Day unto day uttereth speech"[6] becomes real to us in proportion to the light we are able to shed on others in our walks and associations among our fellow humans, and in proportion to our true understanding of the Kingdom of Heaven within; for we can teach others only when we ourselves know.

Night Unto Night Showeth Knowledge

Before light there was darkness, the darkness of our separation from God. In this night souls gained knowledge of universal laws through suffering. A way of redemption was prepared through, and out of, this state of separation. "In him was life; and the life was the light of men. And the light shineth in darkness; and the darkness comprehended it not."[7]

In each of us there is the pattern of the *original state* of separation. With the night, there comes to us an opportunity for rest, reflection, meditation and inspiration; or a time for sin, misery, and mental torture. Just so, in each trying experience of life, night may teach us such a lesson of love and sympathy that we may be changed individuals, or it may harden us, submerge us, until our lives become a burning hell.

Gradually we may learn that life is an opportunity to better understand our relationship with the Father. If our experiences make us more like Him, more kind, more considerate of the fallen, more tolerant of those in authority, they are worthwhile experiences.

The night affords opportunity for us to appreciate the light; for hard experiences show us knowledge. Night is as a film upon which the real may be pictured. In this experience we may obtain a picture of the activity of light and become aware of whether we are making ourselves one with the light or are being held in darkness.

We have within us both light and darkness, and we must make the separation even as God did in the beginning with the whole universe. Creation is going on all the time in us, and we are becoming either children of light or of darkness.

[6]Ps. 19:2   [7]John 1:4, 5

While in darkness, we may become conscious of the light through the light within. It is then possible to realize our opportunity to turn around and come to the appreciation of the light even in the physical. How much more this is possible in the spiritual! "See, I have set before thee this day life and good, and death and evil."[8] "Choose you this day whom ye will serve."[9]

Our spiritual activity must be in the day, in the light, if we would help others; for the night of doubt will come when no one can work. It will be then the time of harvesting that which we have sown.

When the Master was tempted, He did not deny the existence of evil; rather, He recognized it for what it was, and made the separation, saying, "Get thee behind me, Satan."[10] When passing through the great trials of night, we have only to make our wills one with that of the Christ. If we mean this, then the burdens become lighter, the trials easier to bear.

Experiences Regarding Day and Night

There are times when we are very sensitive to the remarks of our friends and loved ones for they seem so unkind. If we study ourselves, we will find that it is we who are out of tune; we have turned away from the light. In this state we unfit ourselves to be channels of blessing to others and bring to ourselves attitudes of doubt and misjudgment. What we see in others is a reflection of that which is within us.

We should come to understand that day is facing the source of Light with a mind that seeks to do His bidding. It is the Christ spirit that comes into our heart to awaken us to our relationships with the source of Light, and that helps us in our associations with others.

"I saw a large light. I recognized it as a manifestation of spirit. It moved toward me and disappeared within my inner self. It made me more aware that my body is the temple of the living God and that I must let my light shine in such a manner as to hasten the day of the Lord."[11]

When we turn ourselves away from God, or good, we are living in the night of our life. There is a constant struggle between the forces of day and the forces of night. We can see readily the misery that it brings to each. All over the world people are

[8]Deut. 30:15   [9]Joshua 24:15   [10]Luke 4:8   [11]P.E.

seeking for something to allay the unrest, turmoil and confusion that exist; if all would only realize that peace must come first within, before it can come without, many problems would be solved. "For as he thinketh in his heart, so is he."[12] The world by its thinking shows its states of consciousness. Such states of consciousness may be as high as the heavens, or so low that all may be lost within darkness.

What may we learn from the night? Have we built our night, or are we suffering that others may see the light? Our Lord was brought "as a lamb to the slaughter, and as a sheep before her shearers is dumb, so he openeth not his mouth"[13] that others might be free. If through suffering we may help others to understanding, we, as the apostle, may rejoice in tribulation, which shall work out for us "a far more exceeding and eternal weight of glory."[14]

I Am—Alpha and Omega

The sum total of the beginning and end of our earthly existence is that we may fully realize that we are one with the Father and worthy to be companions with Him in glory. Day and night, light and darkness, conflict and conquest, love and service, are means to this end. The problems in a life experience can be stepping-stones to greater service in all realms.

"Have ye not known? have ye not heard? hath it not been told you from the beginning? have ye not understood from the foundations of the earth? It is He that sitteth upon the circle of the earth . . . hast thou not heard, that the everlasting God, the Lord, the Creator of the ends of the earth, fainteth not, neither is weary? There is no searching of his understanding."[15]

> [God] is the beginning and the end of that brought into material manifestation, or into that known by man as the plane or dimension from which man reasons in the finite. Then there will be to the body the correct conception of that meant. "I am Alpha and Omega; beginning and the end." That God, the Father, the Spirit, the Ohm, is the influencing force of every activity is not wholly sufficient unto man's salvation, in that he is a free-will being. As intimated that Alpha beginning, Omega ending. For, the confirmation, the segregation, the separation, the building, the adding to it, is necessary—in relation to those activities that

[12]Prov. 23:7 [13]Isaiah 53:7 [14]II Cor. 4:17 [15]Isaiah 40:21, 22, 28

lie between—for man's building to the beginning and the end.

262-55

Our sonship is exhibited in our choice of free will. Always the urge is to press on. As we were one with Him in the beginning, we will be one with Him in the end, through Him who is the Light, the Truth and the Way.

Conclusion

In seeking to become aware of, or conscious of, our relationship with the Creator and to present our bodies as a living sacrifice, wholly acceptable unto Him, we must learn to differentiate between the day and the night side of life; that is, be able to place true values where they belong. To accomplish this a period of supreme testing may be necessary. As we develop toward the light, we imbibe that Divine Wisdom which aids in knowing the Truth.

Our lives must be judged by the results. If the results are peace, harmony, justice, mercy, love, we know the light is shining within; if they are the opposites, then we know that day has not dawned within us.

As we seek, great upheavals may take place in our life. Ideas which we thought had a sure foundation may crumble beneath our feet; that in which we had implicit confidence may prove to be false. Only God is unchangeable. If we live in accord with His divine laws and seek sincerely for the light, obstacles that would hinder us will become stepping-stones to the realization of our fondest desires, while the impurities and dross that would despoil us will be burned out. Such experiences may be hard to endure, but they are very much worthwhile in helping us to attain to that goal toward which we all are striving.

We must not seek selfishly, but with the desire that His will may be done in all things; never with the desire to override, to outwit, or to outdistance others. God knows our possibilities much better than we, and when He sees a place which we can fill acceptably, the way will be opened. Let us give all glory and all praise to Him, the Giver of all good and perfect gifts, for the example of His Son, whom He sent into the world to guide us out of darkness.

The Son's power has not been diminished. His Spirit is

constantly on the watch to guide those who would be guided over the rough and stony path, and to lift up those who stumble and fall. Let us have faith in the Infinite Power of Good, and know that God's plan for the world will never be overthrown. If we choose the dark path, know that He, from the very stones over which we stumble, will raise up others to carry on; for God is not mocked.

"Whither shall I go from thy spirit?
Or whither shall I flee from thy presence?
If I ascend up into heaven, thou art there:
If I make my bed in hell, behold, thou art there.
If I take the wings of the morning,
And dwell in the uttermost parts of the sea;
Even there shall thy hand lead me,
And thy right hand shall hold me.
If I say, Surely the darkness shall cover me;
Even the night shall be light about me.
Yea, the darkness hideth not from thee;
But the night shineth as the day:
The darkness and the light are both alike to thee."[16]

[16]Ps. 139:7-12

Lesson III

GOD, THE FATHER, AND HIS MANIFESTATIONS IN THE EARTH

Affirmation

May the desire of my heart be such that I may become more and more aware of the spirit of the Father, through the Christ, manifesting in me. *262-57*

III

GOD, THE FATHER, AND HIS MANIFESTATIONS IN THE EARTH

[Based on Edgar Cayce readings 262-57 through 262-60]

Introduction

The purpose of this lesson is that there may be known to each of us how, when and in what manner we may be conscious of the spirit manifesting through us in material things. (See 262-60.)

This achievement in a great measure will depend upon the application of the teachings found in our previous lessons. Each lesson is a step in a search for God until we come into full realization of His Presence abiding with us.

The Great Question

What is our concept of God? Is God in our life only a fact, an all-wise, all-inclusive, all-manifesting force, or is He a loving and forgiving Father?

No one deep within oneself doubts that God is a fact. All realize that life itself is a mystery beyond the explanation of the wisest, and that there must be a source from which it springs. People have called this source by many names *but all* have been moved by the intricacy and perfection of the universe. In the minds of many there is no need to seek another state of consciousness, for the Force supplies bountifully the wants of all who labor. It manifests in all things, and at all times; certainly, they say—God is a fact.

Then, how may we come to know God as *our Father?* God is a Father only to those who seek Him. "Ye shall be my people, and I will be your God."[1] So, as we, who apply that which we know of the Father's will, go about thinking—and thinking in such a

[1]Jer. 30:22

161

manner that the words of the mouth and the activity of the hands
bespeak the will of the Father—then, this activity, this thought,
makes us the channel through which the manifestations come.

> For, who may know in the earth the heart of the mother save
> a mother? Who may know the will of the Father, God, save those
> that put into the acts of their hands, in the thoughts of their
> minds, those things that He has given and as He shows forth in
> the experience of all men from day to day?
> So simple, then, is it to know the Father that all stumble in
> that they *think* of themselves more highly than they ought to
> think.   262-58

Instead of seeking to be channels through which the Father
may make His love and His glory manifest in the earth, we often,
in our selfishness, seek our own ends.

> Be rather as a channel through which the Father may make
> His love, His glory, manifest in the earth. *Listen* to the voice
> from within. For, He is very nigh unto each of you, if ye will but
> look *within*. And that thou experienceth with the desire that
> thy self be nothing, that the Father, the Christ, may be glorified
> in the earth, brings to the experience of all the consciousness of
> being a manifestation of the love of the Father to the sons of
> men . . .
> What are the manifestations of the Father? The fruits of the
> spirit. Gentleness, kindness, the loving word, patience, hope,
> persistence, and—above all—consistency in thy acts and in thy
> speech. Be ye glorious in thine activity. Be ye joyous in thy
> words. For, *happy* is the man [who] knoweth that his life
> bespeaks that the Son and the Spirit of Truth directs the words
> and the activities of his body!   262-58

A question which naturally arises is, "How can we interpret
some of the words and acts of others as manifestations of God,
when they hurt us so much?" Condemn not in words, in thoughts
or activity, that you be not condemned. Be angry and sin not. Be
patient, seven times seven forgive; yes, seventy times seven. (See
262-59.)

We should see in every experience of activity of another our
attempt to express, to manifest, our concept of divine reality.
Each one of us as we give expression in thought, or in act, shows
what is the impelling influence in our experience. We must not

be a judge or a faultfinder; but, rather, be merciful to those who err; for they know not what they do.

God, the Father

Do we know God as a loving Father? If we have not had the experience, why are we afraid? Are we too lazy? Are we willing to accept and use the abundance that is set before us, to enjoy the pleasures and bounties of a divinely created world, without a thought of a great Force behind and in all things? This failure to recognize that which is the essence of life, leads us to self-indulgence and self-gratification, whereby we increase the misery of our fellow human beings and bring turmoil and suffering upon ourselves.

To know our relationship with the Father we have to pass often through trials and sufferings. That is not God's way of finding us, but our way of coming into realization that we are on the wrong road. All of our trials have been of our own making. The longer we fail to acknowledge this fact, and fail to do anything about it, the longer we are in coming into our full relationship with the Father. Let us remember that only self stands in our way.

Jesus, the Christ, is the greatest example of the Father's love. Through the teachings presented by the Son, God has shown an understanding of each heart, a willingness to bring peace to each soul that will turn toward Him.

The Manifestations of the Father in the Earth

The children of the Father seek to manifest His spirit in the earth. It is the law. Like begets like.

We are each a corpuscle in the body of God, performing our individual function.

We and God do not measure greatness in the same manner. The truly great are those who have the spirit of love, never those who march to power through the blood of their fellow humans. One seeks for self glory, the other is selfless in glory. As we study the lives of those who, under great difficulties, have expressed the fruits of the spirit, and observe how the world has been made better through their efforts, it should give us courage to do faithfully that which we find to do.

The Master has told us He has gone to the Father; that is, become one in consciousness with the Father; and that whatever we ask in His name, the Father will give to us, that He, the Savior, the Christ, may be glorified in the earth. If we are His we should know that the answers to our prayers are to His Glory, and for our good.

It is often necessary that we be tried as by fire. The fires of the body, the fires of desire, the fires of the flesh, the fires of the carnal forces, must be burned up.

When conditions and circumstances bring experiences to us that try our souls, and we search in anguish for a reason for it all, we may realize a deep and abiding joy and peace in calling to mind the admonition, "Be still, and know that I am God."[2]

When there are those activities in a material world that bring about the forces or influences wherein there may be the action of a soul in its development, it may be often counted to some as sin or error, while in reality it may be only mercy to that soul from an all-wise and beneficent Father, who is directing, planning, giving the soul an opportunity for the use of that which may come into the soul's experience in the material plane. What the soul, through its body and mind and their attributes, does about the knowledge, the consciousness of the indwelling of the spirit of life through the Christ in the earth, is the opportunity for that soul to develop. Therefore, when we condemn, it is a selfish manifestation, and is an attempt, as was the first sin, to blame on another that which we ourselves have done, else we would not recognize it.

Perfect Manifestation in the Earth

If we would know the love of the Father (that has been manifested through His Son, who overcame sin, error, disease, and even death itself in the material plane), then let us rely on the power of His indwelling presence and have a greater knowledge, a greater understanding of the Christ Consciousness, the Christ Life, in our experience.

To accomplish this we do not have to shut ourselves away from our friends, our associates, or even our enemies. The Master never did. If it is our purpose to manifest perfectly the fruits of the Spirit, this is possible through our manner of living. We

---

[2]Ps. 46:10

should seek, therefore, to know His way for us. This cannot be achieved by denying the existence of sin or error. It is true that sin and error are not of God except through our willful disobedience. If there is in us the manifestation of greed, avarice, hate, selfishness, unkindness, ungodliness in our life, they will bring their fruit—contention, strife, hate, avarice, and separateness from the light. Those who have turned their face from the light of God can see only shadows and darkness. Yet, if they will turn to the Father of love as manifested in the earth through the Christ, even in this life there may be seen the light and the glory of a *new* birth. ". . . for His mercy endureth forever."[3]

The Father has not left His children alone, but for every temptation has prepared a way of escape. Should we be less merciful? We were in the beginning made children of God, yet few of us act as His children.

We can understand better perfect manifestation in the earth, when we comprehend, when we realize that there is no time, no space, and that the divinity of the man Jesus was perfect in His own activity in the earth; for it (His sacrifice) was offered even from the first. (See 262-57.)

If we would be perfect manifestations then, let us be ready to forgive, even as our Master did. He did not set any moral law but that of which the soul of humankind was conscious. So, we may know that within dwells the spirit of God, that which quickens if we will acknowledge His power and His divine right with us. When the Master lived among people His presence cleansed all who sought relief from physical disease, and better prepared them to manifest the fruits of the Spirit in their lives. He did not save their bodies from the grave or transition from one sphere to another, but He quickened their souls and their minds to such a degree that they would cry as Joshua of old—" . . . as for me and my house, we will serve the Lord."[4]

Throughout the experience of humanity in the material world, at various seasons and periods, would-be teachers have come; setting up certain forms or certain theories as to manners in which individuals shall control the appetites of the body or of the mind, so as to attain to some particular phase of development.

There has also come a teacher who was bold enough to declare himself as the son of the living God. He set no rules of appetite.

[3]Ps. 118:29   [4]Joshua 24:15

He set no rules of ethics, other than, "whatsoever ye would that men should do to you, do ye even so to them,"[5] and to know, inasmuch as ye do it unto the least of these, thy brethren, ye do it unto thy Maker. He declared that the kingdom of heaven is within each individual, and that each through meditation upon the fact that God is the Father of all could become aware of the kingdom. Such a teacher became the Christ. Here, then, you find a friend, a brother, a companion. As He gave, "I call you not servants . . . but I have called you friends."[6] For, as many as believe, to them He gives power to become the children of God, the Father; joint heirs with this Jesus, the Christ, in the knowledge and in the awareness of this presence abiding ever with those who set this ideal before them.

What, then, is this One as an ideal?

As concerning our fellow human beings, He taught that we should do unto others as we would have them do unto us, to take no thought, to worry not, to be not overanxious about the body, for He knows what things we have need of. Then we should realize that in the place, in the consciousness in which we find ourself, today, is that which is needed for our greater, our better, and more wonderful unfoldment.

But today HEAR His voice, "Come unto me, all ye that labor and are heavy laden, and I will give you rest."[7] The Lord loveth those who put their trust WHOLLY in Him.

This, then, is that attitude of mind that puts away hate, malice, anxiety, jealousy. And in their stead, since mind is the builder, creates the fruits of the spirit; love, patience, mercy, long-suffering, kindness, gentleness. And against these, there is no law. They break down barriers, they bring peace and harmony, they bring the outlook upon life of not finding fault because someone "forgot," someone's judgment was bad, someone was selfish today. These ye can overlook, for so did He.

In His own experience with those whom He had chosen out of the world, if He had held disappointment in their leaving Him to the mercies of an indignant high priest, a determined lawyer and an unjust steward, what would have been thy hope, thy promise today?

[5]Matt. 7:12   [6]John 15:15   [7]Matt. 11:28

We Are Manifestations of God

Let each of us, in our meditations, in our study, in our observations of the concepts in this lesson, make applications of whatever spiritual law we become conscious of through our individual experiences. For, as He taught, we may call Lord, Lord, even may heal the sick, may cast out demons in His name, and yet not be accepted in His sight. The lives of those who make profession of their associations with Him must bring forth manifestations of those things that are of the spirit, of the fruits of the spirit. "Not everyone that saith unto me, Lord, Lord, shall enter into the kingdom of heaven; but he that doeth the will of my Father which is in heaven."[8]

What are the manifestations of the Father in the earth? To do good to all people, to manifest the fruits of the Spirit in our thoughts and in our acts, as we meet our fellow humans in their own conditions where troubles, doubts, fears and distresses assail them. As we manifest the fruits of the Christ, of the Christ Consciousness, in our words, our acts, in our dwelling with others, we will, as the Christ, manifest in the earth good to all, whether they are of His fold or those who reject that which He lived and taught. In this manner the Son manifested the Father in the earth: so in Him we have an example.

As we apply those truths that we know, we will come to those experiences where we may be lamps to the feet of the wayward, an aid to those who seek, a light to those who have gone astray, a guiding hand to those who would know more and more of the love of the Father as it manifests in the acts, the thoughts, the lives of His followers.

What is our light? What is our guide? Have we tried just being kind in order to see how this law operates in the experience of our neighbor?

A smile raised hope; that hope made possible activity; that activity made a haven for some discouraged, disheartened soul.

Let us smile though the heavens fall; though we may become as naught in a world of selfishness, we may rejoice in the light of Him who has given Himself for our redemption.

> Let Him, the Christ, be the guide. Let Him build for thee the mansion, rather than with thine own puny hands where moth and rust doth corrupt and where those that unconsciously in

[8]Matt. 7:21

their stumbling manners oft make the road rough for thee.
Forgive them, if ye would be forgiven. Hold not a grudge, for
that which is thine may not be taken from thee lest *thou alone*
cast it aside by envy, strife, unkind thoughts, unkind acts, and
thus destroy that thou lovest most—*life!*   *262-60*

How long has been the cry, "Hasten, O Lord, the day of Thy
kingdom in the earth," of those who have manifested the glory of
the Father through the Son. What are the promises that the Son
has given? "I go to prepare a place for you . . . that where I am [in
consciousness], there ye may be also."[9] "I will come again, and
receive you unto myself."[10] As we attune our mind and our body-
activity into that consciousness, our desires hasten the day.
While the merciful kindness of the Father has, in the eyes of
many, delayed the coming, and many, as were the children of
Israel, are ready to say, "Make us gods, which shall go before
us."[11] In patience, in listening, in being still, may ye know that
the Lord does all things well. Be not weary that He apparently
prolongs His time, for, as the Master has given, as to the day, no
one knows, not even the Son, but the Father and they to whom
the Father may reveal it. The Son prepared the way that all
people may know the love of the Father in the earth. Into our
keeping, to us His children He has committed the keeping of, the
saving of the world. Then know that as our minds, as our hearts
desire more and more for the glorifying of the Son in the earth,
for the coming of the day of the Lord, He draws very nigh unto us.

Keep thine heart and thine mind singing in the glory of the
manifestations, of the beauty and of the glory of the Father in
the earth, as thou hast seen manifest among men . . .
Keep in the way that thou knowest to do, for He requires not
other than that ye be true to that thou knowest in thine heart
to do. For He calleth those by name that have named the name
of the Christ and that keep His ways, and through such may the
love of the Father, through the Son be manifest in the earth.
262-58
Lead me, O Father, just for today, that I may be used as a
channel of blessing, that I may today manifest Thy love through
my association with those I contact for as I show forth Thy love
in the earth to my fellow man, the promise comes to me that
Thou wilt guide, guard, protect and comfort me in the ways that
I go.   *262-60*

[9]John 14:2-3   [10]John 14:3   [11]Ex. 32:1

Keep ye all in the Way. Be happy. Be joyous. And may love and mercy and peace, that cometh from the Father to those who use themselves in His service, be *with* thee. Amen.   *281-19*

Lesson IV

DESIRE

Affirmation

Father, let Thy desires be my desires. Let my desires, God, be
Thy desires, in spirit and in truth. *262-60*

IV

DESIRE

[Based on Edgar Cayce readings 262-64 through 262-72]

Introduction

Desire originates in the will. It is of the earth and of the spirit. It is activated, in the realms in which it is directed, by that which is the motivating force, through the will and the mental abilities and faculties of the individual. (See 262-64.)

> [Desire] is the basis of evolution, and of life, and of truth. It also takes hold on hell and paves the way for many [who] find themselves oft therein. In spirit, in body, in mind.   *262-60*

Desire is the power which drives our physical, our spiritual self, while will is the directing force. The positions in which we find ourselves are drawn to us through our desires. Whatever we are physically, mentally, or spiritually has been built through desire.

Physical Desires

It is written in the Scriptures, "And the Lord God formed man of the dust of the ground, and breathed into his nostrils the breath of life; and man became a living soul."[1] Biologically, we make ourselves as animals on the physical plane with three primary urges—self-preservation, propagation of the species, and hunger. These three are forces in us and animals that are instincts. If by the force of will we use them for self-aggrandizement, they then become material desires, and are the basis of carnal influences. In so doing we belittle our spiritual or soul body.

The basis of physical desire is adding to, contributing to, or

[1]Gen. 2:7

gathering together, in forces, that which makes for the abilities of each of us to revel in those urges that are of the animal nature. If we are governed by these, there is no recourse for us other than through spirit. Our soul was created as a companion with the Creator, able to become aware of itself, yet with influences that require the spiritualizing of the creative power of will. This develops god-likeness in the soul or activity. (See 262-63.)

> . . . spirit moves in the direction in which it is motivated by will and desire.   *262-64*

Physical desires which are not spiritualized hinder the development of the consciousness of oneness with God.

"I asked in prayer for three things. All of them were physical desires. One was for the protection of the name of the family, one for comfort, one for some work to do. The prayer was answered, but it did not bring either peace or harmony, only discord, trouble and greater responsibility. In whatever place we find ourselves, if we have the Christ spirit, we will have peace."[2]

Mental Desires

Desire is that impulse which makes for activity of the mental body, whether the impulse is produced from the environ that affects the physical organism, or that which arouses the spiritual or soul body to an activity.

Our physical desires that remain carnal in purpose may become powers for evil when strengthened by a mind that is evil in its intent. The mind in humankind, with its ability to make comparisons, to reason, to have reactions through the senses, can be raised to such forces of activity that it creates for us the environs about us, and changes even our hereditary influences.

Our mental desires that are to laud ourselves, to appraise ourselves, above our fellow humans, make it possible for carnal desires to become stumbling blocks in our experiences. It is one of the immutable laws that whatever the mind of a soul dwells upon, that it becomes; for mind is the builder. If our mind is in attunement with the law of force that brought the soul into being, it becomes spiritualized in its activity; if our mind dwells upon or is directed toward carnal influences, then it becomes destructive.

[2]P.E.

Let Thy will, O God, be my desire! Let the desire of my heart,
my body, my mind, be Thy will, O Father, in the experiences
that I may have in the earth!   *262-63*

When we make our lives and activities in accord with the laws
that are manifested in spiritual attributes, we find that we grow
in grace, in knowledge, and in understanding of His ways. Let us
pray, "Lord, use us; let that which Thou seest is best be done in
and through us at this time." Let that mind be in us that was in
Him, who asked nothing for Himself, but went about doing good.

Our purpose and our will stimulate desires that grow and take
hold upon the mind as do habits upon our bodies. Let us again
remind ourselves that our mind is the builder, regardless of
whether it has its inception from spiritual forces or from carnal
forces. If we would grow, we must keep our mind in constructive
channels. We know that the source of all that builds is He who
has declared that He is the way, the truth and the light. The
earth was brought into being by Him. We are His by creation, His
by possession, His through those promises given to the children
of mortals. What is our desire? What will we do with this man
called Christ?

Spiritual Desires

Let us empty ourselves of desires that are physical in purpose,
that our spiritual attitude may be glorified in our walks before
our fellow human beings. Our greater soul development may be
found by losing sight of ourselves, by spiritualizing our material
desires, and by seeking more and more the Christ Consciousness.
In the garden when the Master prayed, "O my Father, if it be
possible, let this cup pass from me; nevertheless not as I will,"[3]
we see the flesh warring with the spirit itself and physical desire
spiritualized.

In making our physical desires one with the will of the Father,
we will pass through conditions in our experience similar to
those of Jesus, who became the Christ. Pray then that His will be
done in us, and through us, that we may desire to be channels of
blessing to others, in the ways and manners that He sees best.
"Not our way, O Lord, but Thy way." This is spiritualizing
physical desires.

In studying desire, we may question in our mind as to whether

[3]Matt. 26:39

it is necessary for us to give up all physical desires in order to develop spiritually. It is not necessary to give them up, but it is necessary to spiritualize them, that our desires may be His desires, and His desires, our desires. "And unto him that smiteth thee on the one cheek offer also the other; and him that taketh away thy cloke forbid not to take thy coat also,"[4] are examples of spiritualizing desire, for in so doing the desire for vengeance becomes spiritualized through love and forgiveness.

This experience is an illustration: "I had reached the place where I must choose whether I should take my place with those who are preparing the way for the coming of His Kingdom, or accept the ease and pleasure the world offered me. It was a great comfort to me to know that the Master had a similar choice to make, and that in love He overcame desires of the flesh. My prayer was, I cannot bear this alone, my Savior, my Christ, I seek thy aid."[5]

The Gospel of Jesus Christ is the gospel of love and forbearance. To be like Him we must spiritualize the desire to get even by doing good to all for His name's sake. We must desire that the Lord will use us as channels of blessing to all whom we contact day by day, and that there may come in our experience whatever is necessary that we may be cleansed completely; for when our soul shines forth in our daily walks, in our conversation, in our thoughts, in our meditation, we spiritualize our desires in the earth.

As He has given, "It must needs be that offences come; but woe to that man by whom the offence cometh!"[6] Let our desires be so unselfish that we may never sin against our fellow human. We must be the arm, the shoulder, the one upon whom some may lean as they come in their experience to the knowledge of the love of Christ.

When we have suffered through the acts of others and can realize that the suffering has made us more gentle, more considerate, when we regard with compassion the one who caused the suffering, and desire that nothing but good may come to that person, then our desire for revenge has been changed into a spiritual desire.

Physical forces are in the material realms of activity. Mental forces are both spiritual and physical in their reaction to the body

---

[4]Luke 6:29   [5]P.E.   [6]Matt. 18:7

and to conditions mental, spiritual and physical which surround us. If our purposes are spiritual, and we hold to them, we are more able to meet and overcome adverse conditions in the material. Every force, every power, that is manifesting as a force in the material has its inception in spirit; and when applications are made of a material nature, they must coordinate with the mental, the spiritual, the physical, in order that greater and better conditions may be manifested in material things.

His mercies are sufficient unto those who put their trust in Him. Has the Father changed? Has He faltered in His promises? He has promised to meet all after the pattern given on the Mount. "Draw nigh to God."[7] " . . . so shall ye be my people, and I will be your God."[8] His children are those whose desires are His desires. When we hold such attitudes we have no fear, for "perfect love casteth out fear."[9]

The Wisdom of Unselfish Desire

If our activities are such as to bring into our experience the satisfaction of selfish interests for fame, fortune, position, and to be well-spoken of, they are physical. If they are such as to bring into our life the desire to express love, patience, long-suffering, gentleness, kindness, service to others, then they make for spiritual development. If we desire to know whether we have chosen wisely, we should ask ourselves, "What is the desire that is being gratified by the attributes of the relationships being sought?" If it is for aggrandizement of self's own physical desires, then it is carnal. If it is for creating a channel for an expression of good, then it is spiritual. As to the choices, these we ourselves must make. What we sow we must reap. Ambition, unless it is tested in God's crucible, is of itself sin. Not that we should not be ambitious—no—but rather ambitious that God should be the guide, and not self.

When we view ourselves either from the spiritual, the mental, or the material plane, we may see reflected in our experience just how we have meted out the knowledge we have known. What we do with our abilities, our opportunities, brings forth fruit in due season. We find ourselves either at peace within, or filled with doubt, fear and consternation. Would we have peace? then let us make life peaceful to those whom we love, to those against whom

[7]James 4:8   [8]Jer. 11:4   [9]I John 4:18

we have a grudge, to those whom we do not care for. If we would have love, then let us be lovable even to those that show, in our own understanding, disregard for His ways. For the events of life are the experiences and expressions of a soul seeking. What in the experience of humanity can be more direful, more dreadful, than to be lost, yet seeking? Fear and trembling assail us, yet— will we let Him in? His spirit maketh our spirit and soul aware of the love of the Father. The toil and strife are for just a little while. We are living now in eternity.

Let praise and honor be in our purpose toward those things that make us aware of His Presence abiding with us; for His promises are sure, and they who walk with Him shall know Him.

The Price must be paid! There is no such thing as receiving without giving. If we would have life we must give life. If we would have joy we must make joy in the lives of others. If we would have peace and harmony we must create peace in self and in our relationships with others. This is the law, for like begets like. We do not gather olives from thistles, or apples from bramble bushes, neither do we find love in hate.

"Let the words of my mouth, and the meditation of my heart, be acceptable in Thy sight, O Lord, my strength and my redeemer."[10] May we in wisdom choose Thy desire to be our desire.

Conclusion

Know that what we choose to do has a constructive influence within ourselves and those about us; else beware. Those things that bring pleasure and ease in material associations in our life are not at fault unless we worship them or use them selfishly. Things of the earth will pass away, but love that sustains in the hour of testing abides with us always. Knowing this, let us keep the earth singing. This can be done as we look deeper into the heart of the rose, listen to the song of the bird, see the paintings of His face in the setting sun, see the loveliness in the moonbeam that turns all into the radiance of His glory, see in the raindrop, the storm, all nature, and even in those ugly things in people's lives, the desire for expressing love rather than hate, harmony rather than discord! As to results, leave them to Him who gives life, who takes life; for "The earth is the Lord's . . . and they that

---

[10]Ps. 19:14

dwell therein."[11] Let us fill our minds with the desire to know that we are the Lord's, and He will work in us and through us, guiding our hands and our feet and our walks in the paths of life, that we may be channels of blessing to all whom we meet.

Come—come! Let us make known our desires in the light of that which has been promised by Him, who is the Light and the Way, to those who seek to know more of the Father's will. Let us make known the desire of the heart, that we may be one with Him. We must not faint at the trials, at the temptations, at the weaknesses; for He has called us. Will we not harken? He is able to fulfill that which He has promised into our material, mental and spiritual experience. Let not evil overcome us, but let us overcome evil in His name.

Each soul goes on from things *terrestrial* to things *celestial,* from things material to things mental and spiritual, and in each of these realms the consciousness of the soul seeks expression in that particular field of activity which it has built within its own inner self. The soul lives on that it may become more and more aware of abiding, and living, and being in the Christ Consciousness.

> Come, my children, ye that seek the Lord; He is nigh unto thee. Thou hast purposed well in thine studies, in thine preparation for those that would seek through these channels to know more of what thy Lord, thy God, would have them to do. Be not satisfied, but rather content in that ye are being a channel of blessing to thy fellow man. Thou are as the leaven that will leaven the whole, for some there be among you that will hear His voice—and He will walk and talk with those that are willing, joyously, that He, thy brother, thy Christ, thy Savior, would direct thy ways. Keep the faith. *262-67*

> Our Father who art in heaven,
>   Hallowed be thy name.
> Thy kingdom come. Thy will be done;
>   as in heaven, so in earth.
> Give us for tomorrow the needs
>   of the body.
> Forget those trespasses as we forgive
>   those that have trespassed and do trespass
>   against us.

[11]Ps. 24:1

Be Thou the guide in the time of
trouble, turmoil and temptation.
Lead us in paths of righteousness
for Thy name's sake.   *378-44*

Come ye children that seek the light! Bow thine heads in
praise to the Son. For, the way for each of you that would seek
His face, is being opened before thee. The Son of Man, the
Christ, thy Lord is among thee even in thine heart—if ye will
but open the door to Him!   *262-63*

Lesson V

DESTINY OF THE MIND

Affirmation

Lord, Thou art my dwelling place! In Thee, O Father, do I trust! Let me see in myself, in my brother, that Thou wouldst bless in Thy Son, Thy gift to me that I might know Thy ways! Thou hast promised, O Father, to hear when Thy children call! Harken, that I may be kept in the way, that I may know the glory of Thy Son as Thou hast promised in Him, that we through Him might have access to Thee! Thou, O God, alone, can save! Thou alone can keep my ways! *262-73*

V

DESTINY OF THE MIND

[Based on Edgar Cayce readings 262-73 through 262-90]

Introduction

We have come, in our search for God, to a point where we enter
a new cycle. The information which we shall now study may be
found by some to be at variance with much that has been
presented by many others. Truth may be proved only by results.
If we would be led by the Spirit that leads into all truth, we may
expect to have many opportunities for proof in our own life. We
alone can judge as to that which is truth for ourselves.

Our next three lessons will be on destiny: Destiny of the Mind,
Destiny of the Body, and Destiny of the Soul. The first lesson,
Destiny of the Mind, deals with mind in its relation to the varied
attributes of the mental, physical and spiritual bodies.

Mind is of God. It was given as a grace to us, *that we, that soul*
might be a companion with, one with, the mind of the Maker.
Therefore, mind, a creative, Godlike force, is impelled by a
spiritual impulse to build an at-one-ness with the Creator. Its
various phases confuse many, yet they are made plain as we
make our mind, our *purpose,* and our *aims* one with our Ideal,
and realize that the Lord our God is one Lord.

Destiny

Destiny is a law, an immutable law, as lasting as that which
brought all into being. It is expressed in all the varied spheres of
manifestation. We see its signs here and there, written in the
experiences of all whom we meet along the way.

Destiny is that immutable law set by Mind, that called into
being worlds, the universe, the earth, humankind. This MIND,

God, gave to us a soul, a portion of Himself, and when we fell away He furnished a channel, a way, an access to the throne of grace, mercy, and truth, through the Son. The soul is that part of us that may be in accord with, in the presence of, the Father. Flesh and blood—until spiritualized as He, the Christ, spiritualized His body—cannot inherit eternal life. However, in the final analysis, the motivative force of each atom of the physical body is the Mind of Creative Energy.

"Heaven and earth shall pass away: but my words shall not pass away."[1] What is this law of destiny? What is this gospel? What is this judgment? What is this truth? Is it summed up in, "For as he thinketh in his heart, so is he"[2] or "And as ye would that men should do to you, do ye also to them likewise,"[3] or is it answered in the new commandment of the Master, "Love one another"?[4] Yes, the whole law is fulfilled in love, in "Thou shalt love thy neighbor as thyself."[5] "The Lord is ... not willing that any should perish, but that all should come to repentance."[6] We wonder, can such be possible in threescore and ten years in the earth? We wonder, does the time of birth, the place of the environment, make or have a part in our destiny? Do the days or the years or the numbers all have their parts? Yes, and more. All these are signs, omens, marks along the way. But these signs do not design a destiny; for destiny of the mind, of the soul, of the body, is in Him. Nothing that we may do develops righteousness (262-75), but it is the mercy of the Father, exemplified in the Son, which provides for the destiny of mind, body, and soul in the endeavors and environs of their experiences. The way is so clear that there need not be any stumbling for those who put their trust in Him.

Let us be mindful; for the day of the Lord draweth nigh to many. While we wonder, let us search our hearts and know, as of old, that faith is counted as righteousness to those who love the Lord. The soul that seeks shall find. The soul that puts into practice day by day that which it knows may the sooner find peace and love in the earth. "And we know that all things work together for good to them that love God, to them who are the called according to his purpose."[7] In such faith we will know that our destiny is in Him.

---

[1]Mark 13:31   [2]Prov. 23:7   [3]Luke 6:31   [4]John 13:34   [5]Rom. 13:9
[6]II Peter 3:9   [7]Rom. 8:28

Mind in Relation to the Mental Body

There is the triune—the mental body, the spiritual or soul body, and the physical body, and these are one. They, in their own spheres of activity, have their attributes, their precepts, and their ideals. What one finds in the physical is a material manifestation of a spiritual import built by the mental aspect. In building the ideals, the mental body, or the mind, builds either from that which is spiritual (and thus everlasting) or from the material import which changes under varied seasons, environments and outlooks in the experiences of life.

In the beginning God created the heaven and earth. The mind of God moved, and matter with form came into being. Mind, then, in God, the Father, is the builder. Mind, in itself, is both material and spiritual. That which finds expression or manifestation in material things is of the physical, for matter is an expression of spirit in motion. That which is expressed or manifested in spirit, without taking body or form is of spirit, yet may be manifested in the experiences of an individual. Mind may function without form or body, but the Ideal is of the unseen Force or Spirit.

So mind is the moving influence that promotes growth within us and makes for expressions in materiality. What is the meaning then of: "For as he thinketh, so is he"?[8] It is in this way that growth comes. In material things, as we shall find as respecting the Destiny of the Body, as one eats so is the physical person. So it is what we continue to think, we become. We destine that which is the growth of influences in our experiences, that which fulfills the purpose for which we came into being, or just the opposite. Not by a thought do we change this or that, but by *constant thinking, constant building.*

Christ came into the world to teach us how to think constructively, in order that we might return to our original estate. "Let this mind be in you, which was also in Christ Jesus, Who . . . thought it not robbery to be equal with God."[9] He lived in the earth, in matter, yet with the mind, with the thought, with the manifestation of Creative Force in every phase of expression. Through God's gift of a free will to the soul, each entity is endowed with the power to use this building force, the mind, to glorify self or find attunement with God.

As we contemplate, as we meditate, we should know what we

[8]Prov. 23:7   [9]Phil. 2:5, 6

are seeking. What is our ideal? What would we have our mind-body become? Let us remember, it becomes that upon which it feeds, either by thought, by assimilation, by activity, by radial force, by atomic influence, or by the influences of activity in any sphere in which it finds itself. Frequently, we are confused in trying to analyze the source of any impulse. We cannot tell whether it comes from the activity of the physical mind or from some indefinite spiritual source. The result is that we are likely to become involved in interpreting the difference in the spiritual import and the physical necessity of such an impulse. What has been set? It is what we do about that which we know which brings growth; for the first movement of mind from the spiritual aspect or from the material aspect is ever a portion of our activity. Therefore let us set our Ideal in Him who shows the way, and know in whom we believe.

Mind in Relation to the Physical Body

Souls chose to manifest in material bodies, and thus mind found an expression in the physical plane. Mind is still the building force. Through the action of the physical mind, our activity, the food we eat, the very contour and expression of our features are gradually molded. We are an organism partaking of all about us.

The question, naturally, is asked: Is the destiny of our mind set at the time of our birth into materiality as to what we shall think, what our environs will be, and what will be the length of our period of expression in the earth? Are we destined to have this or that experience? We should remember that our choice, our wills add to the pattern we are building. This pattern destines that we will pass through experiences that are necessary to give us greater opportunities to become one with that purpose for which we came into being. Thus, that which our mind works at in its thinking, in its purpose, we become. Does this belie that which the Master gave, "Which of you by taking thought can add one cubit unto his stature?"[10] It indicates—rather, assures those who accept what He has given—that it, the thought, the growth is never accomplished through inactivity, but through repeated activity.

Have we then anything to do with our days in the earth? How

[10]Matt. 6:27

do we read? "Honour thy father and thy mother: that thy days may be long upon the land which the Lord thy God giveth thee."[11] Then is it with us? Is it within the gift of the Father? Both, "For in Him we live, and move."[12] If we think and live the life of love in Him that is Life, that is Love, we fulfill that destiny which He has purposed for us.

Mind in Relation to the Soul Body

What we think, what we put our mind to work upon, to live upon, to feed upon, to live with, to abide with, that our soul body becomes. That is the law, as in the beginning each thought of the Creator bore within itself its own fruit. What propagates the species in the seed of the oak, the grass, animal, or the human being? It is the active force that moves within its own realm of activity, giving expression of that first thought of Creative Forces. That is the destiny which the *Easterners* say was set in the beginning. But this is only half a truth; for if the mind dwells upon spiritual things, it follows that it becomes spiritual; if the mind dwells upon self-indulgence, self-aggrandizement, self-exaltation, or selfishness in any of its forms or variations, then it has set itself at variance with the First Cause. Even before we came into matter—the will, through the mind, was at variance with Creative Forces.

This law, "Hear, O Israel; The Lord our God is one Lord,"[13] enabled us to comprehend the true nature of the Father: One, from everlasting to everlasting. When we become constructive in our thinking we create in our experience the knowledge of this oneness. There has been that battle of duality between flesh and spirit from those periods when we first projected ourselves into flesh. While flesh, as all matter, dies in the physical plane, the soul does not; for it is life itself, a gift of God to us, and only in patience may we possess it.

Signs Along the Way

In the earth plane there are certain signs which we may interpret according to individual understanding. They indicate the development reached in the soul's journey through many spheres of experience and point the way to the path chosen by the soul for this present life's expression. It is regarded by many that

[11]Ex. 20:12   [12]Acts 17:28   [13]Mark 12:29

some of these signs are found in the study of astrology, numerology, phrenology, and palmistry. We should exercise great caution in allowing any of these to become the ruling influence in our interpretation of destiny; for they are all subject to the will and indicate only development and possibilities.

Dreams, astrology, numerology, the vibrations from metal, stones, and so on, should be considered only as lights or signs in our experiences. They are as candles that we stumble not in the dark. Worship not the light of the candle; but rather that to which it may guide us in our service. The vibrations of numbers, metals, and stones are merely influences to help us to be in attunement with the Creative Forces. The pitch of a song of praise is not the song nor the message therein, but a helpmeet for those who would find strength in the service of the Lord. So let us use them only to attune ourselves. How? As we apply that which we know, we are given the next step. These do not give the messages! They only attune us so that the Christ Consciousness may give the messages. It is the application that makes for the development in relation to conditions or experiences. The birth on a certain date does not destine this or that. The destiny is only that certain urges may arise, but what we do about them makes for the changes. Each country, state, and town makes its own vibrations by or through the activities of those who live there. Much confusion arises as many of us may try to interpret signs in accordance with the changes in vibrations which have been brought about purely by our will.

In seeking for light let us not confuse the signs with that which is sought, nor confuse the impulses that may arise from inner urges, or from the emotions of the body that take hold upon the spiritual forces, with that which has prompted them. All power, all force, is in Him, and is subject to His will. In Him is the light that we should seek, that we, in body, mind, soul, and purpose, may be one with Him. He is the Way! (See 818-1.)

Do dreams of physical conditions come to pass? Are such conditions set at the time dreamed? Why should we dream of any given conditions? These may be answered for us if we recall that the law of cause and effect is immutable through choice in our experiences. Hence, as our thoughts, purposes, aims and desires are set in motion by mind, their effects are as a condition that IS.

In dreams we attune our minds to those storehouses of experience that we have set in motion. At times there may be the perfect connection, while at others there may be static or interference by our inability to coordinate our own thought with the experience or fact set in motion. The result of a perfect attunement is evidenced in our lives, for some see visions, some are interpreters of the unseen; some are dreamers of dreams, some prophesy, some are healers, some are teachers; yet all is from the same spirit. This may have little reference to destiny, but it has much to do with mind, the soul mind.

Conclusion

We are fellow travelers on the road to God. There are many routes and many ways of transportation from which we may choose. We may be directed along the way by teachers, but no one can show us the whole way except Him who is the Way, and in whose keeping is our destiny.

So, know ye the way; point it out. For, as He has given, though ye come to the altar or to thine church or to thine group or to thine neighbor pleading not for self but for others, and it is that ye may be exalted, that ye may be honored, that ye may be spoken well of, for others; He cannot hear thy petition. Why? Because there has another entered with thee into thy chamber, thy closet, and He, thy God—that answers prayer, that forgives through His Son—is shut out. In His name, then, only; for, as He gave, "They that climb up some other way are thieves and robbers" [they that robbed themselves of attaining perfection through the Way]. [See John 10:1.]

Then, today, will ye not rededicate thyself, thy body, thy soul, to the service of thy God? And He that came has promised, "When ye ask in my name, *that* will be given thee in the earth." Then, do not become impatient that ye are counted in this day as a servant, as an humble worker, as one that is troubled as to food, shelter, or those things that would make thy temporal surroundings the better. For ye grow weary in waiting, but the Lord will not tarry; eternity is long, and in that ye may spend it in those things that are joy and peace and harmony, make thy self sure in Him. How? "As ye do it unto these, my brethren, ye do it unto me." [See Matt. 25:40.] Just being kind! Thy destiny is in *Him*. Are ye taking Him with thee in love into thy associations with thy fellow man, or art thou seeking thy *own* glorification, exaltation, or thine own fame, or that ye may even be well-spoken of. When ye do, ye shut Him away.

Enter thou into thy chamber not made with hands but eternal; for there He has promised to meet thee. There alone may ye meet Him and be guided to those things that will make this life, now, happiness, joy, and understanding.

As ye have received, love ye one another even as He has loved you, who gave up heaven and all its power, all its glory, that thy mind can conceive, and came into the earth in flesh that ye through Him might have the access to the Father, God. In Him there is no variableness or shadow made by turning. Then, neither must thy thoughts or thy acts cause a frown or a shadow upon thy brother—even as He. For He gave, "Be ye perfect, even as thy heavenly Father is perfect." Ye say, "This cannot be done in this house of clay!" Did He? Ye say, "This is too hard for me!" Did He grumble, did He falter? To be sure, He cried, "Father, if it be possible, let this cup pass." Yea, oft will ye cry aloud, even as He. Ye cannot bear the burden alone, but He has promised, and He is faithful, "if ye put thy yoke upon me, *I* will guide you . . ."

Take Him, then, in thy joys, in thy sorrows, in all of thyself; for He alone hath the words of life. *262-77*

Lesson VI

DESTINY OF THE BODY

Affirmation

Lord, use me in *whatever* way or manner that *my* body may be as a living example of Thy love to the brethren of our Lord.

262-84

VI

DESTINY OF THE BODY

[Based on Edgar Cayce readings 262-73 through 262-90]

Introduction

In the physical we have the body, the mind and the soul. Each of these represents a phase of experience or consciousness. Our physical body is that which is manifested in the earth in materiality, that which has taken form. The destiny of the body depends upon us. It is held by some that the body, being of the earth-earthy, is born into the earth, dies and to the earth returns. Yet the pattern has been shown by Him who entered into the earth that we through Him might have life and have it more abundantly, that we, day by day, hour by hour, again and again, may realize the revivifying and the rejuvenating of our bodies, until, as He, we come into the consciousness of the perfect human. This may take many experiences in the earth. How gracious is our God in mercy and patience that He shows toward us! Jesus used the words "abundant life," abundant experiences, to show the extent of God's goodness to His children that they might come to an understanding of their oneness with Him.

The destiny of mind is both material and spiritual. Since mind is the builder, there is a very close relationship between the destiny of the mind and the destiny of the physical body. It is through the mind that the destiny of the body is gradually builded. With God rests the destiny of the soul, with us the destiny of the physical body, through the gradual building process of our mind working in and through our physical consciousness. It should be the aim and purpose of our conscious mental activity, therefore, to bring our thinking, which directs the control of our physical body, into accord with the higher purposes of the spiritual mind.

We have each been given stewardship over a portion of life. May we so live that we may say, as the Master, "Of that thou gavest me, O Father, I have lost nothing."

What Is the Physical Body?

Our physical body is an atomic structure, subject to the laws of our environment, our heredity and our soul development. Each atom, each corpuscle, has the whole pattern of the universe within its structure. Our body is made up of elements of various natures that keep it in motion and sustain its equilibrium. It is the channel, the house, the piece of clay, that is the dwelling place of the soul.

The mental body, the soul body, and the physical body are shadows of the Triune. The body-physical is as human, the body-mental is as the savior of humanity; for it is through the application of the mental influences that we control and build that which finds expression both in the physical and in the soul. The soul-body is as of the Creator, for it, the soul, was made in the image of its Creator, to be His companion in spirit. That the physical is the home of the soul during its sojourn in the material world is evinced to all who think about it; what we do with the opportunities that are presented to us in our varied experiences one with another is for each of us to determine.

Are We Aware of the Destiny of the Physical Body?

Our body is the temple of the living God, of the living soul. Is it to see corruption? Is it to be lost entirely, or is it to be glorified, spiritualized? As our body is a structure in which we manifest as a portion of the whole, so our body is in the keeping of its Keeper, even within us. What will we do with it? God gave us free wills. God Himself does not know what we will destine to do with ourselves, else would He have repented that He made us? God has not ordained that any soul should perish. What of the body? Have we ordained, have we so lived, have we made our temple so untenable, that we do not care to have it glorified?

We attempt to adorn our body for our fellow humans. Do we care less for our God? Do we purge the body, as He has given, that it may be made holy for a dwelling place for our soul? What it becomes depends upon that which we do with our opportunities. If we would be like Him, then we must so live, so conduct ourselves, that our body may be one with Him, and be raised a glorified body to be known as our own!

That we may be called by a different name in each experience may be confusing to many; yet when we say Creative Force, God, Jehovah, Yah, Abba, do we not mean one and the same thing? Always we carry throughout various experiences of our consciousness the desire (if we seek aright) to be one with Him, to know ourselves to be ourselves and yet one with the great I Am. The destiny of our body, then, lies with us, and what we do with it in one experience or many experiences is of our choosing.

What Is Meant by Presenting
Our Bodies a Living Sacrifice?

We should present ourselves as channels of blessings for others. To be a blessing may demand that we present ourselves as a living sacrifice, as a living example to others; yet we should understand that sacrifice does not necessarily mean a giving up, rather it is the glorifying of the body for a definite purpose, for an ideal, for a love.

Thus may we in presenting our bodies, through the application of that which we know, show a way in which others may see the initiation necessary for awakening a purposefulness in their experience. It will turn hate into love, strife into peace. Our thoughts, too, have their activity in the experience of all and create the environ, the atmosphere, from which others often draw that which will be the motivating influence in their experiences.

We have each been given stewardship over a portion of life (God). May we be living examples of the things that Christ, the Master, taught and lived. When He calls upon us to render service to others, shall we answer, "Here am I," even though it appears to others that we are laid on the altar of sacrifice? To those who love His ways it is only a reasonable service.

How Shall We Use This
Holy Temple, Which Is Our Body?

"For as he thinketh in his heart, so is he."[1] Then we should take heed how we think; for thoughts are things and may become

---

[1]Prov. 23:7

either crimes or miracles in our lives. It is with right thinking and right acting that we keep the holy temple pure. He stands at the door and knocks. It is necessary to keep our temple clean, so that nothing can enter that will in any way defile or defame the abiding place of the Most High.

Keep the temple silent. Let not the noise or confusion of the world make us afraid, or in any way interfere with our worship. It is possible to be in the world and yet not of the world. Let love alone enter and find an abiding place, that we may become as He, who first loved us.

The pattern has been shown by HIM who entered into the earth that we might have an example. If we would be like HIM, then we must conduct our life so that a glorified body to be known as our very own may be raised. To accomplish this, our mind and our body must be purged so that we may know the glory of HIM who took His own body and so glorified it that it became a pattern for all.

Let the spirit of the Christ guide us from within, and the way will be shown to us. No greater awareness can be had than that which comes when He, who is the Maker, the Author, the Finisher of Life, comes and abides with us.

May we never think that the opportunity has passed; for God's mercy is without limit. We make the choice when we realize that TODAY is the acceptable day of the Lord! It is never too late for us to begin, for life in physical experiences is a continuous effort for making the way in a material world, whereby we may justify ourselves before the throne of grace. Inasmuch as ye do it through love, through kindness, unto the least of these, my little ones, ye do it unto Me, is the manner in which it is accomplished.

All things are possible with God. Do not expect results in a day; for we do not sow one day and reap the next, but we reap what we have sown in the periods when that which is sown comes to fruitage. Indiscretions and sentiments that are based wholly upon material satisfactions, must bring to us tares and weeds in the experience of our body. Those things sown in mercy, truth, and justice will bring their rewards in the same realm, in the same coin that has been sown; for God is not mocked.

If we do our best, we need not worry about results. We can leave the results with our Maker. Let us do right, not merely to be seen of others, but that the glory of the Father may be reflected through our kindness, patience, and brotherly love. These activities beget health, harmony and understanding.

Let us be sure our brother, our servant, yea, our neighbor think as well of us as we think of ourselves! If they do not, it is because sin lies at our door. This does not mean that we should condemn ourselves; for we know that we are God's handiwork, and should act accordingly.

We should know in our heart that what is done in secret must be proclaimed from the mountaintop in our own experience. Even though justice or retribution be delayed a thousand years, we must meet that which we have sown. How will we ever meet it? In the strength of ourselves? Rather may we harken to the promise, "So shall ye be my people, and I will be your God."[2]

What shall we do with this holy temple, this body? Purify it, glorify it, that it may be of priceless value when returned to its Maker.

What Is Meant by the Resurrection of the Body?

The body that we have taken from matter has assumed various forms, sizes, and colors. Hence, with what body shall we be raised?

> The same body ye had from the beginning! or the same body that has been thine throughout the ages! else how could it be individual? The *physical*, the dust, dissolves; yes. But when it is condensed again, what is it? The *same* body. It does not beget a different body!   262-86

We have one wavelength that is ours. We have one light beam, and on it we must come in, must go back to the Father, or else lose our identity. Then we must seek to purge the body until it is raised a glorified body to be one with the Whole, and yet be our own. In other words: to know ourselves to be ourselves, yet one with God. He is not the God of the dead, but of the living.

Our Lord resurrected and quickened His body. He is our pattern. So we, as He, must overcome death, overcome that transition, overcome that which is the conscious change of being in all matters, all phases, all experiences, that we may be one with Him, as He is one with the Whole.

[2]Jer. 11:4

How Should We Regard the
Experiences of the Physical Body?

What we are today is a result of the way and manner in which we have used the opportunities given to us by God, the Father. When we do not take into account our relation to the First Cause, God, we know those things that pertain to the gratification of material desires, that so often turn and rend us. The seed of every plant is within itself; the seed of every living influence is within itself. So in our acts in relation to our fellow human beings and to the world as a whole, the results that will be in our experiences are according to that which we have sown, or the manner in which we have dealt with our fellow human beings.

It is through activity that we may become more and more aware of how we use our opportunities. If we practice error, then error becomes more and more prominent in our dealing with others. If our activity is selfless, then we become like Him who gave Himself for the world. In whatever way we prepare ourself then the time and place to use that prepared will come.

Let the light of His countenance guide us. He, our Lord, is willing, if we use our body, our mind, our abilities, as channels of expression for Him. As known or experienced by those in the material plane, or in any plane of consciousness, those abilities that are manifested are the outgrowth of the application of opportunities by an individual entity in this or that experience. Then it may be seen that in aiding others there comes greater aid to us; for it becomes a part of ourselves and a portion of our own experience.

The purpose for which our soul chose to come into this earth plane was to awaken the Divine within, which is done through manifesting the fruits of the spirit toward our fellow humans. Then we should do with our might what our hands find to do, leaving the results in the hands of Him who gives the increase. Let us look upon every experience as a necessary element in our own development, knowing that He who clothes the fowls of the air and the lilies of the field will be mindful of those who love His ways.

All in matter, all in form, first began in the urge of mental or spiritual influence, and that which prompted them came into manifestation under the influence of divine guidance. That which is error, that which is shame, that which is of disrupting forces, become negligible unless given power by thought, and by activity of the mind. Not that denying alone makes for nonexistence, but rather that those things presenting themselves as errors, as a disrupting influence, may be used as stepping-stones for the creation of those environs in which we may change trial, temptation and hardships, into helpful experiences: for through the things which He suffered and overcame He became the King of kings, the Lord of lords. So with us it may be found that by using our experiences rightly there may be brought into our consciousness harmony, which is another name for peace, for good, for joy. For while flesh and blood that is of the earth may not gain or know glory, the body, the real body—not the superficial, but the real body—may become aware of itself in the Presence of the body of God, among its brethren, and a portion of the Whole.

Let us keep our innate faith in the oneness of power in Creative Forces; and as we express it in our activities with our fellow humans, as we hold it in our meditation, as we hold it in our mind, so will it be experienced in our inner self. All must pass under the rod, but He has tempered it with mercy and judgment. So must we temper our judgments, so must we find patience, so must we find those things within self that make for the answer to us before the Throne of grace. If we would have mercy, we must show mercy to our fellow human beings, yes, to our enemies, to those who despitefully use us.

Death in the flesh is a birth into the realm of another experience, to those who so live that they are not bound by earthly ties. This does not mean that we do not have our own experience in and about the earth, for we come into the earth plane for the purpose of further development toward a cooperative, coordinating activity with the Creative Force that manifests through our activities in materiality. In the earth the choice is by will, while in the interim, between the earthly incarnations, the choice is conditioned by that which has been accomplished by us in manifested form; for we must meet that which we have sown in the body.

How May We Show Ourselves Approved?

Our bodies are only channels through which our souls may manifest the attributes of the spirit of truth in a physical plane.

We find ourselves in that state where we are subject to the faults, the failures, the conditions, that work upon our weaknesses. These may work through environmental and hereditary influences or through associations, yet there is the awareness in our experiences that God, Creative Force, has prepared the way of escape from those things that so easily beset us, if we call upon Him in sincerity. Our activities are our voluntary choice. We have been given the manner, the way in which the Christ Consciousness is manifested in the earth, through Jesus. He came as man that through His example, love, patience, and hope might be shown. This He exemplified in His activity, that we might choose, as He, to do that which is right, just, sincere, and honest, in our activities one with another. "Inasmuch as ye have done it unto one of the least of these my brethren, ye have done it unto me."[3]

The way is simple. Yet those who would seek through the mysteries of nature, the mysteries of the manifestations of life in the earth, or those who would see the activities of their neighbors, friends, or associates, rather than listen to that which may be had through the still small voice from within, become troubled and wondering, and then fearful, until there come periods when the sureness of self is lacking.

What are the requirements then, that we may become aware of His presence abiding with us? They are that we manifest love, patience, hope, charity, tolerance, and faith in our daily life. These words, these expressions, these as visualized objects may be within us, and when we make such manifest in conversation, in example, in precept to those whom we meet day by day, we become aware of the Christ Consciousness.

Know the truth for the truth's sake. "Heaven and earth shall pass away: but my words shall not pass away."[4] Let not, then, the cares of the world, the deceitfulness of riches, pomp, glory, or fame, hinder us from applying in our relationship with our fellow humans those laws through which we may become aware of His presence.

That offences must come, is true, but woe to them who bring them to pass!

May we not be idle in doing that which we know to be right. Let our activities be positive, our love be without dissimulation.

[3]Matt. 25:40   [4]Mark 13:31

"Abhor that which is evil; cleave to that which is good."[5]

As we have seen in our own body that which has brought the fires of nature, the turmoils of disease, the wonderments even of distress, and as we have seen those influences, those powers, in nature that are manifestations of His love to others, we know that in our weakness, in our strength, on Him alone we can lean for strength. He has prepared a way. We, in any phase of our experience, are only the channels to make application, or to give helpful understanding to others. His abiding presence is in and with us.

The destiny of the body lies with us. We can take only a perfect body back to our Maker. (See 696-3.)

[5]Rom. 12:9

Lesson VII

DESTINY OF THE SOUL

Affirmation

Lord, let me—my mind, my body, my soul—be at-one with Thee: that I—through Thy promises in Him, Thy Son—may know Thee more and more. *262-88*

VII

DESTINY OF THE SOUL

[Based on Edgar Cayce readings 262-73 through 262-90]

Introduction

Humanity in its natural state is soul. In the beginning all souls were created in the image of the Creator. Thus the first creation was spiritual.

The development of our souls in a material world is as a garment that is made up of the warp and woof of materials that we have gathered through our experiences in every plane of consciousness. In our sojourns in the earth, we wear many kinds of garments—working clothes, prison garbs, and wedding gowns. Just so we build into our souls, through our mind directed by our will, that which is Godlike and uplifting, or selfish and degrading. That which we build within our soul gives it the opportunity for occupying a position of honor or dishonor. Through the will, however, we may make those things that are of dishonor as stepping-stones to positions of honor. This, too, makes its mark on the soul. Our will is a divine attribute; how we use it determines our destiny. Each soul is an offspring of Creative Force of GOD, and is innately the result of the manner in which it has manifested the prerogative of WILL.

Let us strive to understand that life in its essence is spiritual force, and is continuous. The point of expression may be in matter, as here on earth, or in any of the many different planes of consciousness, but mind is the universal moving force which acts and builds through all planes, and gradually brings an awareness of our own individuality *in that Creative Force we worship as God.*

Creation of Soul

The soul is of God. It had its beginning in God and its ending is only in Him. To name the name of God is to recognize that we are a part of the Whole, and we know, because we are of the Whole. Our soul, as a part of Creative Force, came into being, and was given breath, by the will of the Father, that it might be a companion with Him in His activity. Our soul is everlasting, containing eternal creative power, and through expressions of this power we may come to know ourselves to be one with Him. Then the destiny of the soul, as of all creation, is to become one with the Creator.

The entity is the manifestation of soul in spiritual, mental, and physical form. Though our soul may have wandered far afield, though it may make its bed in hell, though it may take the wings of the morning and fly to the utmost parts of the universe, eventually it must wend its way back to the source from whence it came, to its God, its Maker.[1]

Our soul never dies. How can Spirit die? How can God die? How can God destroy Himself? Though our soul may choose to take up body after body, though it may seek experience in this or that sphere of consciousness, it is ever seeking the way back from whence it came. What is the origin of the soul? What is the origin of eternity? Eternity is from everlasting to everlasting. "When the morning stars sang together"[2]—we were there. When the heavens fold up and time will be no more, behold—we will be there. Now, as in the beginning, we are children of God, and our destiny is to be rulers and priests and priestesses unto Him.

The Soul's Association with the Mind and the Body

The soul body is the image of the Creator, a companion in spirit with the Creative Force. It is too wonderful to describe. It, as God, must be experienced to be known. Our physical body is simply a temporary house for our soul. Opportunities are presented to us through physical experiences for using and directing the soul powers lent to us by God. The way we use these powers in relation with others shows the concept or degree of awareness of our attunement with God.

Through sojourns in the earth our soul, through will, brings upon itself many experiences that may result in confusion,

[1] See Ps. 139:8, 9　　[2] Job 38:7

turmoil and strife, or a better understanding of the purposes of life. For example, if we consider that slights, slurs, and unkind words are directed against us, and we remain untouched within and can rise above the selfish desire to strike back, then we can understand what Jesus taught as He urged us to seek attunement with the Father. Jesus overcame in this way and knew that we, too, could rise above being hurt, or tempted, or mistreated. With Him as the pattern there is within us no desire to strike back. Each time we resent, we add to these confusing urges that become stumbling blocks for us. Thus we may use those things that have hindered, that would cause the quickness of speech, the anger at being thwarted, as stepping-stones to a more perfect understanding and to a realization of being in accord with His Way.

As we give our selves, our love, our patience, and our kindness, however hard it may be, to help others, we learn His Way and may depend upon His help to sustain us. If we let the beauty of His life guide us, then those things that beset as a temptation, those things that make us afraid, may be cast upon Him, who has promised to bear our burdens with us.

It is well that we understand that our soul takes on physical bodies as means through which practical applications can be made of tenets that make for the development of our soul. Such opportunities arise in our dealings with our fellow humans. Our entrance into the earth plane at any time is for the purpose that another lesson may be gained, another opportunity for soul expression may be had. Our knowledge of a law is not sufficient within itself, but when knowledge is made active and practical, it then becomes a moving force in our lives. Let us seek to make our bodies channels through which Creative Energy may become an *active* force, whereby we may gradually become aware of our own identity in the Creator.

We may become *aware of our soul* through commonplace, everyday observance of spiritual laws within our understanding, by putting into daily application the laws of love and service to others. We must measure up to that which we hold as the ideal in our relationships with our fellow human beings, for we can estimate our concept of God by examining our attitude toward others.

Jesus meant what He said when He told us to seek first the Kingdom of God—then all things might be added, but they are added only when we are in harmony with those around us. Then it is in patience with self, in patience with our friend, in patience with our foe, that we become aware of our souls. These are the manners, these be the ways, in which we may know that there is an access to the Father through the Son.

No soul has been left without access to the throne of mercy and grace. The promise has been given, "If ye love me, keep my commandments. And I will pray the Father, and he shall give you another Comforter."[3] Though there may be periods of trial and temptation, when our purposes seem fraught with disappointments, if our faith has been placed in Him we may find that which will help us grow in understanding and knowledge of His love; for whether in the body or out we are His manifestation.

The soul's association with mind and body is the greatest of earth's experiences, but to spiritualize all three and make them one in Christ is the work of a Master. That is our privilege.

The Activities of the Soul in the Material

It is not knowledge, nor is it understanding, but the application of the opportunities that present themselves, that builds the destinies that arise in the experience of our soul. A law is not set and our soul set adrift upon the sea of time or space. There is something that we must do, and there is always the presence of the Father to sustain us. He has promised, moreover, to meet us in the Holy of Holies, and He is not slack concerning His promises.

Let us study, then, to show ourselves approved unto those promptings that come from meeting the Divine within, and be able to say we know in whom we have believed, and know that He is able to keep that which we have committed unto Him in every experience that may arise. The spirit that prompts our activities in a material world arises within the soul and is expressed in our dealings with our fellow human beings; therefore, we cannot hate our neighbor and love our God; we cannot worship our God and hold malice against our neighbor, for these are of One Force, and the law of One is perfect.

If we sow in spirit, our mind builds that which we reap in

[3]John 14:15, 16

spiritual values; if we sow in materiality, our mind builds that which is of the earth-earthy. Let us put our ideal in spiritual things and know that as we mete unto our neighbors, so will it be meted unto us. In our relationships to our fellow human beings, let us act in such a way that we may always look ourselves in the face and not be ashamed to have accorded to us whatever we have accorded to our neighbor; for we must meet ourselves.

Let us keep an attitude of sincerity, of oneness of purpose; for if we are sincere with self, and most of all, sincere with our fellow humans, we will not fear to be called into the presence of our God. Thou, O Lord, art holy in Thy dealings with Thy children. O God, we are Yours in body, mind, and soul! Purge us, that we may be one with You, and through that power that You have given us, may we make known to others the beauty and the love that You have showered upon Your children, should be our prayer.

Do we have one standard for self, and another for our friends, for our relations, for those about us? All are one in Him. If we would have peace, mercy and grace shown us, we must show them to others, for in so doing we become aware of the indwelling of His presence.

If we use our knowledge to gain the advantage over others, or to lord over them, what must be the destiny of our soul? The Master gave, "For whosoever shall give you a cup of water to drink in my name, because ye belong to Christ . . .he shall not lose his reward."[4] It is not, then, in mighty deeds of valor, or in those things that bring fame or fortune, it is not in the things of high estate, that the greatest soul development comes, but rather the growth comes as line upon line, precept upon precept, here a little, there a little, through kindness, love, patience, scattered along the way. Such growth in spirit brings true knowledge and true understanding of the purposes of a soul's indwelling in the earth; and this understanding helps us to realize that unless that which we do is for the good of others, it must eventually fail; unless our activities among others are to aid the greater number, rather than classes, they are of little benefit to ourselves or others. For, true indeed, they that knoweth to do good and doeth it not, to them it is evil. They that know not and do evil, to them the Father may give countenance; but they that know evil and do it, to them it is damnation.

4Mark 9:41

Our soul must meet itself and give an account of its activity in the earth. What we do in the physical we meet in the physical, what we do in the mental we meet in the mental, what we do in the spirit we meet in spirit. "Whatsoever a man soweth, that shall he also reap."[5] When we know to do good and do it, we make our life worthwhile. After all, it is just being gentle, though others are harsh, just being true, though others are false, just being patient, though others about us are impatient. If we are on the Lord's side, who can be against us? (See 696-3.) We find ourselves in that which we have built; so, to do good, let us use that which we have in hand; the environments and experiences that make for changes that are necessary in our life will present themselves. If the preparation is made, the time and place to use our knowledge will come about. It is the law; it is His love. (See 991-1.)

Conclusion

Let our choice for development mean more and more seeking to be in at-onement with God, the Creative Activity within our experience. For each expression of our soul in any phase of its experience may, through works, through thoughts, and through activity, become a channel of expression of the Creative Force in the material world. This is the natural growth, the purpose for which we entered into every experience, that there may be the greater expression of God through us.

Finally, the destiny of our soul is in Him who gave the soul, that we (our soul) might know, might be one with that Creative Force we call God. The manner in which we use opportunities makes for either consternation, turmoil, strife or just the opposite. How has God meted judgments to us? Not other than in the manner in which we have shown mercy. What will we do with this man, our elder brother, our Christ, that our destiny might be sure in Him? He has shown us the more excellent way: not in mighty deeds of valor, not in the exaltation of knowledge or power, but in the gentleness of spirit—love, kindness, peace, long-suffering, patience. These, as Jesus has shown, must be applied in our associations with our fellow human beings day by day. There is nothing in heaven, in earth, or in hell, that can separate us from the love of God, save ourselves. (See 849-11.)

[5]Gal. 6:7

Then the exaltation of ourselves, of our abilities, of our powers, of our indulgences, must be lost in gentleness and in patience; for it is only in patience that we become aware of our soul. When our individuality is lost in Him, our personality shines as that which is motivated by the individuality of our Lord and Master. Thus does the individuality and the Destiny of the soul lie in the keeping of Him who has given Himself in the world that we may know everlasting life. He has given that if we abide in the Father, "I will bring to your remembrance those things from the *foundations* of the *earth,* from the foundations of the world, that ye may be where *I am;* and thy glory in my glory, in thy God, shall make of thee that oneness that passeth understanding of men who see only a mental-material consciousness." (849-11)

> "There will come a day in which all who dare
> May see the Lord.
> And those who put on the robes of righteousness
> May rest in peace.
> And those who have come up through great
>   tribulations
> Will fear no more;
> For the King of Glory, on the brow of the blessed
> Will place a diadem
> And great joy will fill the heaven and the earth,
> For death will be no more."　　　　　　　　P.E.

Lesson VIII
GLORY

Affirmation

Open Thou mine eyes, *O God*, that I may *know* the glory Thou hast prepared for me.   *262-89*

VIII

GLORY

[Based on Edgar Cayce readings 262-90 through 262-95]

Introduction

In the interpretation of Glory, we sometimes let conditions disturb us; therefore, we often get an incorrect understanding of it. GLORY IS OUR ABILITY TO SERVE, which is an opportunity given to us by God. When Glory is considered from the phase that God has chosen us above our fellow humans for some special work, then vainglory may creep in. All are called into service; God is no respector of persons. Our ability and our service begin with cooperation in being channels through which the glory of the Lord may be manifested in the earth.

Glory, then, in all phases of our experience, as related to Creative Force in manifestation in the earth, is to be studied with conditions that deal with our fellow human beings. Then, if we would fill the place for which we have been called, we would let our glory, our knowledge, our wisdom, be in the Lord; for our glory is only a reflection of the glory of the Creator. It shines on us and through us as we become channels through which blessings may come to others.

The manifestations of God are varied; yet in purpose He is the same yesterday, today, and forever. In our spiritual ideal, purpose, and aim we, too, should be unchangeable. Our activities may be varied, but they should always be expressions of the glory of our spiritual purpose; that is, expressions of our oneness with the Father. "If a man love me, he will keep my words: and my Father will love him, and we will come unto him, and make our abode with him."[1] Such is glory.

[1]John 14:23

Glory of the Mind

"As a man thinketh in his heart, so is he."[2] Unless our mind is stayed in Him, the giver of life and light, we may find ourselves chasing shadows in our search for glory. The mind is ever the builder. With our minds firmly fixed on our Ideal, who always lost sight of Himself, we may find glory in service by using our minds to build within us knowledge and wisdom that will fit us for greater opportunities—not to the glory of self, but to the glory of God. It is indeed a glorious thing to be constantly in the hands of the living God and to know that no matter how difficult the problem is, it will be solved eventually in the right way.

To accomplish this, our ideal must be beyond the purely material things in life. Those things that are of the earth rust and corrupt, but those ideals that are founded in the spirit of life and truth take hold upon the very throne of mercy, peace, and harmony, and build within us an understanding of long-suffering and love of others.

That which is impractical and theoretical is of little value. Oft we have heard that we should not let our good be evilly spoken of.[3] This may occur if we speak one way and live another. Oft we proclaim in our experience that we believe this or that, and then proceed to act differently. Then such activities become stumbling blocks. What is the law? Like attracts like! "Purify thy body, physically. Sanctify thy body, as the laws were given of old, for on the morrow thy God would speak with thee!" (281-13) How do we interpret such a promise? If we believe this, we should do something about it; for it is not what we declare that we have attained, but how willing we are to be used in practical and helpful service for our fellow humans.

Jeroboam made the children of Israel sin when he offered the sandalwoods of the Egyptians. He only aroused passions within himself, when he should have made his offering to the GLORY of the Lord. (See 274-10.) So may we, for self-glory, for the approval of others, offer to our Lord that which may bring our destruction.

When we have put off the glory of self-exaltation and put on the glory of God, conditions, circumstances, environs are no longer stumbling blocks but become stepping-stones in our development.

The earth is a school for those who in the beginning erred through self-indulgence, self-aggrandizement, self-glorification.

---

[2]Prov. 23:7   [3]See Rom. 14:16

It is, indeed, a merciful experience then; even though we find turmoils, strife, antagonism, and disturbing forces in our experience, we have opportunities through which we may be cleansed, and may become channels through which a GLORIFIED Father IN the Son may be manifested in and among humans.

We should take into serious consideration the fact that animosities or hard feelings held against others create in the mental forces of our bodies that which may easily become very destructive influences. Our outlook, and the way we worship that which we hold as our Ideal, have much to do with our physical reactions. Our mind, let us remember, is of our mental, physical, and spiritual bodies, and it can either create or destroy.

If there is built within our mental forces the attitude that there is a hindrance that blocks us in any manner, it gradually becomes a barrier, limiting the efficiency of both our body and mind. In our inner self, in our mind and heart, let us be aware of that given of old: There is set before us good and evil, life and death. (See Deut. 30:19.) We are given the choice. (See 815-3.)

Glory of the Body

May we never lose sight of that which is the whole purpose of the body. The body is the dwelling place of the soul, which through the mind expresses itself in materiality.

The actions of our body are one with Creative Energy . . . so long as we perform acts of helpfulness, of love, of patience, and of kindness; but when we seek the gratification of selfish desires and the exaltation of self, we become one with forces that bring doubts and fears. As we in any experience express the fruits of the spirit of a living God, we grow, unfold, and manifest the purpose for which we were created.

What is evil? It is good misapplied, good used to satisfy the desires of self. So is sin, so is illness. They are caused by not being at-one with God, who helps us, while in the body, to become a force for good and a perfect channel for the manifestation of righteousness among all. The glory of the body, then, is selflessness.

Glory of the Soul

Our soul is a portion of the Divine. It is a moving influence in our activities throughout our experiences in all spheres of consciousness. Our soul is a universe within self. Will is an attribute of the soul, and with it we choose to develop either to a oneness with Universal Consciousness or in opposition to it.

The three phases of our human experience—body, mind, soul—are expressed in the earth, and their freedom comes in a threefold manner through knowledge, interpretation, and application. All of these work together and depend each upon the other. In service, without thought of personal gain, comes that which makes for the greater growth of our soul. "He that is greatest among you shall be your servant."[4] Our physical, mental and spiritual bodies—each in its own phase of expression—must find, from experience, that which will keep them in accord with the purposes for which they entered into physical being.

Why are we pulled by the material, mental, and spiritual urges, while always something deep within keeps us trying to go forward? What is it that makes us KNOW that we must fight through obstacles and that will not let us give up? Are we fools that we keep working at something without any apparent material recompense, simply because we are urged from within? Why don't we give up, stop trying, and just let things and conditions run their course? Would not the final material results be the same? These questions often war within us. There is deep within us always the answer. The material results might be the same in the end; but what about the effect on our soul?

Do we want to be guided by His Spirit, to be a portion of that Word which shall not pass away? If so, then indeed we are right to respond to the urge from within to "carry on," even though everything seems to contradict the practicality of doing so. He has given that we should not mind those things that will destroy the body, but those that will destroy the spirit and the soul. Even though all material things may be swept way, if we still have that urge from within, we are in touch with a glory which may not be found in any material substance or relationship.

Conclusion

In our dealings with our fellow human beings, let the law of the LORD, as we know it in our hearts, be the rule of our lives; and we will find that the growth of the mind-spiritual, the mind-mental, the mind-physical, will bring the glory of the Lord in our

[4]Matt. 23:11

lives. God has promised to meet us within our holy temple, our body, as we purpose to give ourselves in service to our fellow humans; for in so doing we manifest the Glory of God in a material world. Let the Glory of the Father, of the Son, suffice us—not what we think, or what we say; for people look on the outward appearance, but God looks on the heart. (See I Sam. 16:7.) In seeking to magnify Thy name, Thy glory, through that which Thou dost make manifest in me, O Lord, be Thou the guide, and—day by day, as the opportunity is given—let my hands, my mind, my body, do what Thou wouldst have me do as Thine own in the earth; and as I manifest through Thy love, the promises that Thou hast made in the Son, may Thy glory become known to others.

Lesson IX

KNOWLEDGE

Affirmation

Let the knowledge of the Lord
So permeate my being that
There is less and less of self,
More and more of God,
In my dealings with my fellow man;
That the Christ may be in all,
Through all, in His name. *262-95*

IX

KNOWLEDGE

[Based on Edgar Cayce readings 262-95 through 262-99]

Introduction

Seeking for knowledge has led us into the intricate tangle of physical existence. When the call, "Where art thou?" came to Adam, it brought the realization that God-given powers of creative thinking had been misused. Then fear and doubt became entrenched within our heart.

The first "don't" was: "But of the tree of the knowledge of good and evil, thou shalt not eat of it: for in the day that thou eatest thereof thou shalt surely die."[1] Adam in his weakness made the choice which led him into tribulation, toil, and misunderstanding, for he did not choose the knowledge of good, but he chose the selfish use of the divine power of creative thought, which brought to him confusion, destruction and death. Humankind (a spiritual being), taking things into its own hands, still makes itself ridiculous in the eyes of its Maker by flaunting its knowledge of things that be, not even knowing that they have always been.

What is true knowledge? We have knowledge when we seek to express less and less of self and more and more of God in our dealings with our fellow human beings; for the expression of self is that which hinders us in gaining knowledge of the more perfect way. True knowledge is of God, not apart from God. It is shown fully in our unselfish dealings with our fellow humans day by day, as we manifest the spirit that we care, that we understand, and that we are willing to take a portion of their burden when they are bowed down with the cares of the world. It is being willing for Christ's sake to aid those in distress, to feed those who are hungry. The world is crying for this knowledge.

[1]Gen. 2:17

223

Knowledge is the ability that enables us to live in harmony with the laws of the universe. This again is known to us when we become selfless, and rid ourselves of the little differences that breed hate, contempt, and those things that hurt our fellow humans in our dealings with them. Do we understand that to forgive is knowledge, to be friendly is knowledge, to be selfless in the midst of a selfish world is knowledge? It takes an understanding of only one law to do these things, and this law is love.

Knowledge Is of God

God is Light and in Him there is no darkness at all. The Father judges us by our activities. We dwell then in the light as we study to show ourselves approved unto Him and are workers who are not ashamed of the things that will prove our sincerity and our earnestness. We know that as God is the Author of knowledge, He is the Supreme Judge of all, and that when we judge our fellow humans we are assuming the office of the Lord. "Who hath directed the Spirit of the Lord, or being his counsellor hath taught him? With whom took he counsel, and who instructed him, and taught him in the path of judgment, and taught him knowledge, and shewed to him the way of understanding?"[2]

Knowledge Is Power

Knowledge is power, yet power may become an influence that brings evil, when it is not used constructively. Hence, let us become more and more aware of the desire to be the channels through whom God may carry out His will. Secular knowledge is man-made. The knowledge of God does not bind us to dogmas, or man-made beliefs; rather it sets us free.

Worldly knowledge causes many to become faint, many to fall away. Have we emptied ourselves of tradition, of malice and of hate? Do we encourage the weak, strengthen the fainthearted, and know that in such activities we gain a more perfect knowledge of God's way? In such application of knowledge we will find an understanding of ourselves, and learn to interpret ourselves in our relation to others, as well as in our relation to God.

In our study of the needs for cooperation we found the following statement: "Gaining an understanding of the laws that pertain

[2]Isaiah 40:13-14

to right living in all its phases makes our minds in attune with Creative Forces,"[3] which are in His Consciousness. One of the first of these laws is to know ourselves. In our lesson "Know Thyself," we approach the study of the physical body as a part of our own being. Here, in our lesson "Knowledge," we must turn to a study of the body as it relates to, and indeed pictures, the universe. We should know of the functioning of the organs which are constantly carrying on the processes of digestion, assimilation, and reconstruction of tissue, but it is more important that we should know something of the creative powers that operate through the spiritual centers. Such knowledge is power; for unless our knowledge brings to us as individuals an understanding of a regenerated life and an ability to live with others, we are failing to fulfill our destiny.

Interpretation of Self

Through the study of spiritual forces we learn that before we can know the world without, we must first know the world within. The physical person is of the earth; the soul—with the mind of the infinite—is of the universe. Souls choose to take physical bodies, and thus mind, which is of God, finds an expression in the physical.

Thus the study of self becomes our first consideration if we would be a good neighbor, a good parent, a good friend; and this means to look within to see if we have the knowledge that will help us to walk in the way of Him who is the Way, and to serve others, who as ourselves are made in His image.

Mind is defined as the rational faculty of humanity. It may be divided for convenience into the conscious, the subconscious, and the superconscious. We must not confuse the unconscious mind with the subconscious. The unconscious is but a deeper portion of our conscious thinking, through which the subconscious operates in the physical and acts upon and affects the conscious mind. It is through the mind that creative forces seek activity, whether in a lowly organism seeking to express itself, in us seeking a kingdom for ourselves, or in a soul seeking its way back to God. It is with the mind of the soul that we can be consciously aware that our physical body is the temple of the living God. With the will we choose for ourselves that activity which will either

[3]*A Search for God,* Book I, p. 20

take us away from or to our Creator. It is active in both our conscious and subconscious minds. In the one it brings the ability to reason inductively and deductively, in the other to transcend and know, even as we are known.

Finally we turn to a brief study of the nature of our spiritual self. It has been said that the individual who would seek God must first believe that He is. It was Jesus who taught that the kingdom of God is within our own being.[4] The God-spark within each of us is the force that enables us to love our enemies, to do good to them who persecute us, to pray for them who despitefully use us. Of ourselves we can do nothing; with Him we can do all things.

Our soul, a creation of the Father, constantly desires to glorify Him. Though we stumble blindly at times and often fall, yet, through suffering, we grow to understand and to give expression of our soul purpose by becoming channels through which the Father's will may be done in us.

Perhaps we have been afraid to "let go" and be absolutely happy. Whenever things have been almost perfect we would always think that it wouldn't last, that something would come to spoil it. This should not be our attitude. Although worldly cares and trials may be around us, when the question comes "Where art thou?" we should be ready to answer, "Here am I, Lord, use me."[5]

We may often wonder in analyzing ourselves if we are right in what we believe, if we really know God, and if we have knowledge of Him that we can give to others. There is an answer: If we would know God, we must experience God; and as we experience Him, we become a guide to someone else. This should be to us the answer to every problem.

The Application of Knowledge

Knowledge, divine knowledge, that we had in the beginning, is needed in the affairs of our life. If we had only known the motive which prompted the act, the cause which brought about the unpleasant experience in the life of our neighbor, the severe test and trial which our wayward friend was experiencing, how differently we would have acted! Let us remember that to be kind is acting as if with foreknowledge. We never forget the one who

[4]See Luke 17:21   [5]See Isaiah 6:8; P.E.

understands us when we fail in the discharge of our duty. How like the Master is that one to us! Kindness is a simple act, but it is great enough to express divine knowledge.

> Education is only the manner or the way [to reach the final goal]. Do not confuse the manner or the way with that of doing what ye *do* know! Not when there is a more convenient season, or "When I have attained unto a greater understanding I will do this or that." Knowledge, understanding, is using, then, that thou hast in hand. Not to thine own knowledge but that all hope, power, trust, faith, knowledge and understanding are in Him. Do that thou knowest to do *today*, as He would have thee do it, *in thine understanding!* Then tomorrow will be shown thee for that day! For as He has given, *today* ye may know the Lord! *Now*, if ye will but open thine heart, thine mind, the understanding and knowledge will come! 262-89

What is applicable to an individual is applicable to groups. It is like leaven; it leavens the whole. In groups, we will find differences of opinion, of thought, of interpretation, of development. We do not have true knowledge if we let such differences cause us to judge one another. The way of the Lord is hard only for those who become so fixed in ideas that they are not willing to be led by the Spirit of the Christ.

Knowledge must be applied in the affairs of nations. Have the World Wars made the world safe for democracy? Why not? Doubtless those who were trained in worldly knowledge felt confident that arms, power, and force were the things needed to bring about a Utopian condition. We, the nations, have to learn that the principles of peace and equal rights for all must come first in the hearts of individuals. They must begin with us. We cannot legislate goodness into the hearts of others while we live a life of selfishness.

It has been given that we shall love the Lord our God with all our heart, our soul, our mind, and our neighbor as ourselves. This is the basis of all spiritual law. Safety is founded in the knowledge of the spirit of truth, and the right application of that knowledge is just as effective in bringing its blessings to nations, as the misuse of it is in bringing about confusions among them.

Knowledge of universal laws brings clearer concepts of the purpose of creation. Without knowledge of that purpose we would have no reason for existence. We know that the misuse of knowledge will wreck individuals as well as groups or nations. If we persist in the misuse, then that which seems to be worthwhile will fade, and spiritual decay will follow. Consider the person who worships money, the mob that takes law into its own hands, the nation that wars upon its neighbor; all in time reap that which they have sown.

Correct Evaluation of Knowledge

What experiences do we hold most sacred in our lives? Are they not such as the smile of someone we love, the thoughtful act of a friend, a kindness in time of trouble, a word of praise when things seem to be going wrong? Such knowledge brings spiritual growth. Worldly pleasures and physical gratifications bring excitement for the moment, but they do not last.

A kind word under trying circumstances not only creates for us an attunement with the "I Am" but makes others aware of the presence of the Lord. Our responsibility in applying the correct evaluation of knowledge cannot be overlooked. We should study to show self more practical in the application of that which we hold to be true. But if there are question marks here or there as to our sincerity and our consideration of others, trouble and discord will arise, bringing distressing experiences in our activities.

We are continually meeting ourselves. Would we have disappointments if we had not disappointed someone? Would we be despitefully used if we had not within us some grudge or unkind thought of someone? The law is, that which we sow we shall reap. Though the heavens fall, the law will never change, for like begets like. Knowledge assures us of success; that is, if our purpose is in the Lord and not in our self. Knowledge used aright bears the fruit of the spirit.

No soul, no mind, can comprehend anything beyond its own understanding. Understanding is made perfect in virtue, and virtue is of God. Do we have it? If so, we see the Christ in others, and are filled with love, kindness and peace. To us is given the means to secure that which we need, not in doing someone else's job or attempting to do God's job, but in doing our own. This brings success that fills us with the fullness of a perfect life.

Knowledge of His Presence

We have been told to "Be still and know that I am God!"[6] Do we ever try to pray and know that we are only uttering words? What is the trouble? Have we stepped aside, out of the strait and narrow way, and left God out of our life until we feel alone? God never breaks down doors to get in. He stands at the door and knocks. He is not past finding out, and with Him we can do all things; for His presence brings power and assurance into our lives. Then let the love of the Christ surround us, and let us glory in knowledge that we walk with Him, and that He sustains and strengthens us day by day.

Let us take no thought for tomorrow; for in His presence we shall find strength for each trial, each disturbance. He has promised that He has given His angels charge concerning us.

We must stand fast in Him, knowing, believing, acting that which we profess.

> As ye have received, as ye are moved, as ye apply that ye receive, give to those that seek. Be patient, be kind. Speak not unkindly of anyone. Let not gossip nor unkind things, either in thought or deed, be in thine experience. And ye will find the true Knowledge of the Christ in the Father being close to thee.
>
> *262-98*

---

[6] Ps. 46:10

Lesson X

WISDOM

Affirmation

Our Father, our God, may the light of Thy wisdom, of Thy strength, of Thy power, guide—as we would apply ourselves in Thy service for others. In His Name we seek.   *262-102*

X

WISDOM

[Based on Edgar Cayce readings 262-102 through 262-106]

Introduction

Wisdom is the ability to use knowledge aright. It is made practical by the application of the Christ life in our daily experiences.

> *This* then is not a thing afar off. Not that ye would say as of old, who will bring down from heaven a message that we may know Wisdom, or who will come from over the sea that we may hear and understand; for Lo, it is in thine own heart; it is within thine own power, yea within thine own might! [See Deut. 30:11-14.]
>
> *262-104*

The fear of the Lord is the beginning of wisdom. Not the fear of disappointment, of contention, of strife; for they are not of God. The wisdom of the Lord is exemplified for us in the life of Jesus who became the Christ; then, if we would have wisdom, we must abide in Him who is the Way. Have we been disappointed? Have our wishes, our desires failed to be fulfilled? We still are conquerors; for in Him we have strength and power and might. Let us remember "that all things work together for good to them that love God, to them who are the called according to His purpose."[1]

Our Lord taught that: If thy neighbor smite thee, turn the other cheek; if one takes away thy coat, let that one have thy cloak also; if someone forces thee to go one mile, go with that person two. In such teaching there is wisdom, for we are not hindered by the act, while our neighbor is blessed by being in the presence of the Divine. Nothing except the spirit of God within us

[1]Romans 8:28

233

can make us love our enemies. Do we say in our heart, "Yes, but this was the teaching of the Son of God, and He had the strength that is not within me"? We have the promise of the Son, "Lo, I am with you alway,"[2] and through Him may do greater things than He did.

They that giveth a cup of water in the name of the Christ lose not their reward. It is not wisdom to give it that we may be well-spoken of, but rather that the glory of the Father may be made manifest. It is to the glory of the Father when love prompts the activity, when love prompts the desire to be a blessing to others. Then, we are co-workers with Him. This is wisdom, the wisdom that is of God.

Wisdom is first a matter of choice, of will in the light of that which is our ideal, and in the manner in which we apply it in our experience with others. The concept, the will, the application become a triune in the experience of each of us. If, however, in the application we become selfless, exalt the Prince of Peace, and seek the glory of the Father, we will find ourselves in His consciousness. This is the true approach; this is the beginning of wisdom. Knowledge of the fear of God is the beginning of wisdom. The whole law is to love God with all our mind, our body, our soul—and our neighbor as ourself; that He, the Father, in the Son may be exalted.

We are commanded to use that which we have in hand and more will be given to meet our needs, whether they are mental, material, or spiritual.

The Approach to Wisdom

Ye [would not have] known sin unless the Son had come and shown thee the Way. [See John 15:22.]   *262-104*

He is the pattern of perfection. We, as He, in seeking to know the wisdom of the Father, are brought to an understanding through patience, long-suffering, and love of others. The knowledge of God, the wisdom of God, applied in our daily experience bring strength and harmony; even the turmoils of the earth—sorrow, shame, want, and degradation—become worthwhile experiences, if we meet them in the wisdom of God.

Where strife, turmoil, self-glory and self-exaltation are, there is no true wisdom of God. If we would have love, then we must

[2]Matt. 28:20

show love; if we would have peace, we must be peaceable; if we would bring about a greater and closer association with the Divine, we must so act that there be no questioning in the minds of others as to our purpose in life. There is no shortcut to wisdom; it must be lived.

Let Us Examine Ourselves

We must become more aware that we cannot bear the crosses of life alone, and that the Father in His wisdom has given to us an example, a promise, a friend, a sharer of all our crosses; even the Son of man, who learned through experience . . . what it meant to bear a cross.

> In wisdom, thou wilt not find fault. In wisdom, thou wilt not condemn any. In wisdom, thou wilt not cherish grudges. In wisdom thou wilt love those, even those that despitefully use thee; even those that speak unkindly.   *262-105*

When we claim the promises of God, many changes that we cannot understand may take place in our lives. These experiences may help us to know the Wisdom of God.

When we profess with our mouth that which we have purposed in our heart to do, that is wisdom. When the acts of the body, when the thoughts of the mind are in accord with that we proclaim to our children, our neighbors, our friends, that is wisdom.

"When I lost my home with most of my earthly possessions, a struggle went on within me. I was disappointed with myself for not being able to rise above the conditions that enveloped me. I was disappointed with my friends, who appeared so indifferent to my sufferings. My usual hopeful attitude slowly slipped from me. How I longed to be comforted! I tried to realize that this experience was for my good, and that it was God's way to teach me patience.

"It took this experience to help me understand, and realize that we learn obedience through suffering."[3]

> Then make thy paths straight. Let thy conversation, thy wishes, thy desires be rather as one with Him who thought it not robbery to be equal with God.
>
> Ye know the way. Do ye stumble in ignorance or in selfishness? Do ye doubt for the gratifying of thy body or for the fulfilling of the body-appetites?

[3]P.E.

Ye know the way. Let, then, that love of the Infinite fire thee
to action, to *doing!* And indeed live as hath been shown.

                                                    262-105

Our applications of these truths should be practical in our
everyday life, and not merely tenets or sayings that pass away. As
we live them, they become living, enduring realities. Remember, to
obtain wisdom we must apply that which we know.

Application of Wisdom

In our seeking for wisdom we come to the place where our will,
the faculties of our mind, the faculties of our spiritual forces,
must be divinely directed, if we would go on in the correct
application of knowledge.

Wisdom is divine love manifested in our conversation, in our
avocation, in all our acts.

> For as ye apply day by day that ye know, then is the next step,
> the next act, the next experience, shown thee. Because thou
> hast then failed here or there, do not say, "Oh, I cannot—I am
> weak." To be sure, thou art weak in self, but O ye of little faith!
> For He is thy STRENGTH! *THAT* is Wisdom!
>
> Let no *one* then again ever say *"I cannot."* It's rather, if ye do,
> saying "I WILL not—I want MY way." This is foolishness; and
> ye know the Way. For He is Strength, He is Love, He is
> Patience, He is Knowledge, He is Wisdom.
>
> Claim ALL of these, then, *in HIM!* For He is in thee, and the
> Father hath not desired that any soul should perish but hath
> prepared a way of escape, a way of love, of peace, of harmony,
> for every soul—if ye will but claim same, live same, in Him.
>
>   *262-104*

Would we have wisdom without preparation? Would we have
glory without purification? Would we enjoy happiness without
being able to comprehend and understand it? How may we make
a practical application of wisdom? JUST GO THE WHOLE WAY
WITH OUR MASTER. We should not preach that which we do
not ourselves practice. We should not insist upon others trying
in their experience that which we have not tried.

> TRY in thine own experience, each; that ye speak not for *one*
> *whole day* unkindly of any; that ye say not a harsh word to any;
> about any; and see what a day would bring to you . . . *262-106*

"I dreamed that I was with a great company of people. We seemed to be in the temple at Jerusalem. I was to make pictures of the people. Later Jesus and some of His followers came in, but not through the door that we had entered. He, too, came to have His picture made. He said to me, 'You can make the picture of Jesus, but can you make the picture of the Christ?'

"Then I knew that the picture of Christ could only be reflected to my fellow humans by the life I lived. And so it is with each of us; we know the Christ and introduce Him to our neighbors by the way we speak, the way we think, the way we act. To apply that which we know to be good is wisdom. To love the Lord our God with all our hearts, all our minds and all our souls and our neighbors as ourselves is wisdom, and when anything less is practiced, it brings into our experience sin and sorrow and finally death."[4]

Then the practical application of the Christ-life in thy daily experience is Wisdom indeed.

This then is not a thing afar off. Not that ye would say as of old, who will bring down from heaven a message that we may know Wisdom, or who will come from over the sea that we may hear and understand; for Lo, it is in thine own heart; it is within thine own power, yea within thine own might!

It is the application of that *thou knowest* to do in light of the Pattern set in the Christ. *That* is applied wisdom!   *262-104*

[4]P.E.

Lesson XI
HAPPINESS

Affirmation

Our Father, our God, in my own consciousness let me find happiness in the love of Thee, for the love I bear toward my fellow man. Let my life, my words, my deeds, bring the joy and happiness of the Lord in Jesus to each I meet day by day.

262-106

XI

HAPPINESS

[Based on Edgar Cayce readings 262-107 through 262-112]

What Is Happiness?

Happiness is abiding in Infinite Love. To be happy we must make Infinite Love compatible with our material surroundings. No one can give it to us, no one can take it away. We manifest it in thankfulness, peace, harmony, and in a consciousness that is void of offense toward God and others. Happiness is knowing, being in touch with, and manifesting divine love in our daily life. Happiness is as much a law as error or goodness, as day or night. The first law is: Like begets like. That which we think, we become. As in the act, as in the seed, so in the full fruit of that which we allow our mind to dwell upon, that we become. Happy are they who love the Lord's way. (See 262-109.)

Who Are Happy?

Happy are the poor in spirit, for they shall see God. We are happy when we in humility realize the goodness of the Father, the depth of His love, and allow ourselves to be directed by the God-Force. But when we become acquainted with "familiar spirits,"[1] we dishonor the God who has promised to abide with us always.

Happy are they that mourn, for they shall be comforted. We have a thirst for spiritual satisfaction that only the Spirit of God can supply. We have an advocate with the Father God, in Jesus Christ, and in such knowledge we have comfort. Though we may feel sorrow for others in their unrighteousness, yet we are happy when we can bless those whom our Lord smiles upon in their weaknesses.

[1]See I Sam. 28:7

Happy are the meek, for they shall inherit the earth. "Not by might, nor by power, but by my spirit, saith the Lord."[2] The unseen forces are working the great changes in the earth and its people today. Those who are quiet, cool and unpretentious are the makers and the keepers of the coming age who will bring light and understanding to many. Blessed are those who, without thought of self, go forward, build homes, hospitals, cities, that generations to come may be blessed. These are they who inherit the earth. What we give away, we have, is as true as what we hold, we lose, or what we have lost was never ours.

Happy are they who do hunger and thirst after righteousness, for they shall be filled. "Ask, and it shall be given you; seek, and ye shall find."[3] It is a fearful thing for us to be at ease, to feel self-sufficient and not to realize that we, of ourselves, can do nothing. It is glorious to come to an understanding of our relationship with our Heavenly Father and with our fellow human beings. We are happy who realize that the fountain of knowledge, of peace and of righteousness is overflowing, and that our thirst can be forever satisfied in Him who is the Water of Life.

Happy are the merciful, for they shall obtain mercy. Father, "forgive us our debts, as we forgive our debtors." If we forgive not our neighbors their trespasses, how can we hope to be forgiven? To forgive and to be merciful are Godlike. To hold grudges, to want revenge, to pout and to sulk, are of the earth, and they have no part in the Kingdom of the Father. Happy are the merciful, for they have the promise that their needs will be met.

Happy are the pure in heart, for they shall see God. Unless ye become as a little child, ye shall not see the Kingdom of God. There is no evil in the mind of a little child. The prisoner before the bar is to the child a good person. Unless we, too, can see God in our fellow human being, we will never see Him elsewhere. This is our first step toward God, and there is no roundabout way. There is no happiness within us when we are holding an impure thought of another.

Happy are the peacemakers, for they shall be called the children of God. "Peace I leave with you, my peace I give unto you: not as the world giveth, give I unto you. Let not your heart be troubled, neither let it be afraid."[4] In the world of uneasiness and turmoils, this is a happy state of consciousness; yet peace will not

[2]Zech. 4:6   [3]Matt. 7:7   [4]John 14:27

remain long within if there is no effort to express it without.

Happy are they who are persecuted for righteousness' sake, for theirs is the kingdom of heaven. "And if any man will sue thee at the law, and take away thy coat, let him have thy cloke also."[5] This is another way of saying that we should go all the way in being kind and gentle to others. Because we have little, do we often say that we must save, so that we may not be in want? Let us remember that there may be those who now need what little we hold. We may say, if I were so and so, oh, how much I would give to charity, to the needy! If we would not share the little we have, we would not give although we had everything at our command.

When we are persecuted for righteousness' sake and are conscious that it is for His sake, the light which brings happiness shines into the darkest corner of our life. When we can realize that the place we fill and the work we do is not only a livelihood, but a means through which others may come to a better understanding of life, then the little slurs, the insults, the criticisms lose much of the sting they would otherwise carry. Love comes more easily and forgiveness is given before it is asked, when we are happy to suffer for righteousness' sake.

Happy are you "when men shall revile you, and persecute you, and shall say all manner of evil against you falsely, for my sake. Rejoice, and be exceeding glad: . . . for so persecuted they the prophets which were before you."[6] "They shall put you out of the synagogues: yea, the time cometh, that whosoever killeth you will think that he doeth God service."[7]

When Are We Happy?

When the Lord's will becomes our will, we are happy, for we begin to know the Lord in our daily life. Do we think that Jesus went happily to the cross, or that He went happily from the garden where there had been apparently so little consideration of what the moment meant as He wrestled with self? With all the sadness that this experience gave Him, He was happy in knowing that He would show the world a way out of sin. Do we worry over the shortcomings of those we love? How was He with those He loved? He gave them only His blessings, never His censure. As we follow His example we are happy.

[5]Matt. 5:40   [6]Matt. 5:11-12   [7]John 16:2

Moments of discouragement will arise in our experience. We may expect them; such seem necessary for our training. It need be that offenses come, but woe to that one by whom they come. Let mercy and patience keep each of us lest we forget our opportunities.

Happiness is found in the mind and heart of those who without thought of self seek to know the way of God. It cannot be bought. It cannot be learned. It must be earned. No one can take it from us, but we may, through misuse, lose it. Let our daily prayer be:

> Our Father, our God, in my own consciousness let me find happiness in the love of Thee, for the love I bear toward my fellow man. Let my life, my words, my deeds, bring the joy and happiness of the Lord in Jesus to each I meet day by day.
>
> *262-106*

Pleasure Is Not Happiness

How often we confuse pleasure with happiness. We see those of the world seemingly enjoying every pleasure that luxury can give, yet many have sad faces and heavy hearts.

Pleasure is of the world; it is something outside of us. It is fleeting, deceiving and unsatisfying. It gives no reward but asks a heavy toll as we pass over the bridge of unrealized dreams. Solomon declared, "I made me great works; I builded me houses; I planted me vineyards: I made me gardens and orchards, and I planted trees in them of all kind of fruits . . . Then I looked on all the works that my hands had wrought, and on the labor that I had labored to do: and . . . then I saw that wisdom excelleth folly, as far as light excelleth darkness."[8]

"For what is a man profited, if he shall gain the whole world, and lose his own soul? or what shall a man give in exchange for his soul?"[9]

Let us think on the difference between pleasure and happiness, for they are as the material and the spiritual. Through pleasure we seek to gratify physical desires, but when we have lost sight of self in the appreciation of love, beauty and hope in the Creative Forces, may we indeed know happiness.

The road to Gethsemane, to the minds of those who looked upon their own Gethsemane, was a road of thorns. Yet the Lord's kind words, spoken on the way to His Calvary, brought happiness

[8]Eccles. 2:4-13   [9]Matt. 16:26

to a dying world. "Peace I leave with you, my peace I give unto you; not as the world giveth, give I unto you. Let not your heart be troubled, neither let it be afraid."[10]

Happiness is found in Infinite and Divine Love. Infinite Love is the love of God. Love Divine is that manifested by those who in their activities are guided by infinite love. They are one in Him. They bring happiness, not mere pleasure as is found in material things.

We should find happiness in just sowing the seed. Some will fall on stony ground, to be sure; some by the wayside, some among the thorns and briars; but many will fall on good soil. Then we must keep the faith, knowing that God gives the increase.

We must show ourselves worthy of Him who will guide us in our daily activities. Our greatest opportunities for service are found in being kind, speaking gently, and smiling often. Let the love of the Father through such activities shine in our life day by day. Then the clouds of doubt will dissipate.

If we put first things first, with the proper evaluation of material, mental, and spiritual forces, our life will be a life of harmony, happiness, and joy. Others will be aware of our relationships to our God as we patiently sow the seeds of love.

Conclusion

Truth brings freedom, and freedom brings happiness. "Ye shall know the truth, and the truth shall make you free."[11] In truth we do not bind others, neither do we exalt self.

Selfishness is the only sin. All others are just modifications of the expression of the ego. So close is the ego, the I am, to the Great I Am, that the confusions of duties and privileges and opportunities become enmeshed in our experiences. Many of us in the turmoils of life have lost sight of the proper evaluation of our activities in our relationship to individuals as well as to groups, and fail to consider it our duty to give the help which might enable others to overcome sorrow, fear or worry.

Then if we would have life, we must give life; if we would have friends, we must be friendly. In fields of activity let us draw nigh unto that which is good and think not only of material gains, but of how great a service we may be to our fellow human being! For in so doing we serve our Maker. (See 257-182.)

[10]John 14:27   [11]John 8:32

Lesson XII

SPIRIT

Affirmation

Father, God, in Thy mercy, in Thy love, be Thou with us now. For we know and we speak of Thy love. And help us then to put away, for the hour, the cares of this life; that we may know in truth that the Spirit and the Lamb say, "Come." Let them that hear also say, "Come." Let all that will, come and drink of the water of life.   *262-113*

XII

SPIRIT

[Based on Edgar Cayce readings 262-113 through 262-124]

Introduction

Spirit is FIRST CAUSE, the essence of Creative Power, the source of light, and the motivating influence of all life. It is God.

Let us not be confused by terms. What are the relationships among such terms as: The spirit of the times, the spirit of the age, the spirit of America, the spirit of '76, the spirit of the pioneer, the spirit of Fascism, the spirit of the earth, the spirit of the departed, the spirit of the church, the spirit of Truth, the Spirit of the Christ, the SPIRIT OF GOD?

It has been given that there is One Spirit. All manifestations of life in any plane of consciousness are crystallizations by Spirit.

When we, through exercising free will, choose to misdirect and divert this power into selfish channels of personal aggrandizement, rather than toward the expression of its original impulse, the glorification of the Creator, then sin comes into existence.

The spirit of the pioneer need not signify cruelty and destruction nor the spirit of strife and hate, but spirit beings encased in the physical seeking freedom as an ideal. All force is one force. It is we who brought diversity of expression and perception, and we through the Way must return to unity. "Get thee behind me, Satan . . . for thou savourest not the things that be of God [the Spirit], but those that be of men."[1] These words were spoken by Jesus, when two ways were before Him: self-glory, or the glory of God.

We must understand why and how Spirit came into material manifestation. Where did we come from?

---

[1] Matt. 16:23

> . . . we must know from whence we came, how, why, and
> whence we go—and why.   262-114

In the Beginning

God created us in His image, spiritual beings, with souls, minds and wills. In all states of consciousness there are opportunities for the expression of these.

Error came into existence before the earth, the heavens, or space were created. Using free will, expressing selfish desire, spiritual beings (souls) separated themselves from a consciousness of Oneness with Creative Will. Life, in material bodies, is the reflection of this separation in this state of consciousness.

Through the law of love, God prepared a way back (a road, a ladder, a knotted rope) for all humankind. Until this way was prepared there was no consciousness of time or space. These concepts are aids, not hindrances, to a clearer perception of the Divine Will; for through time and space, and patience, we will come to know the Lighted Path.

Only those who seek may find this way. Flesh and blood may not reveal the truth to us. It is the quickening of the Divine Spirit within which brings each personal revelation.

Humanity's Projection

The Children of God became the children of men, as they sought selfish expression into the earth plane. They pushed themselves into matter, upsetting existent patterns of evolution going on in the earth; first, as forces seeking expression through the natural elements of mineral, plant and animal life, then, as hardened thought forms molded after the pattern of animal life in the earth. In these thought forms spiritual beings became entangled. They lost the consciousness of their divine origin. Monstrosities resulted. There was chaos. The darkness which existed is beyond the comprehension of the finite mind. The earth plane was only a three-dimensional point of expression for the chaotic state which existed.

God's Projection

Out of this mire of selfish thought, this morass of illusion, God prepared a way through the law of love.

He said, "Let there be light."[2] Let there be the consciousness of time and space. The evening and the morning were the first day, a day of light and darkness, of good and evil. Step by step spiritual beings became aware that they were away from God, from Light.

Jesus, as the first Adam, became the symbol of the regenerated spiritual beings returning to God Consciousness. He came showing the way of patience by which we (spiritual beings) were to recognize His state and turn toward the Light. The law of One was manifested eventually in the man Jesus, and is signified in the Christ Consciousness. (Let us get the difference.)

Adam and Eve, God's projection, began a line of physical descent through which spiritual beings could purify their desires, and return to God Consciousness. This is the true source of the legends of the chosen race, the pure race, preserved in the legends of the peoples of every continent.

In the early days spiritual beings who used these Adamic bodies were tempted and many gave way to desire. " ... the sons of God saw the daughters of men that they were fair; and they took them wives of all which they chose."[3]

Down through the ages there existed side by side the sons and daughters of mortals (the hardened thought forms mingled with animal bodies) and the Sons and Daughters of God (offspring of the Adamic race).

Through the example set by the Christ, we know the way. The choice is made daily by each soul to follow the Light or seek selfish gratification. Now, as in the beginning, each individual is meeting himself or herself. When we act without thought as to motive or purpose, experiences result which may bring ease and comforts for a time, but when our activities are selfish indulgences and suppressions of our fellow humans, we will reap that which we have sown.

As we were created for companionship with the Father, being a portion of First Cause, it behooves us in materiality to manifest more and more our awareness of this relationship in our mental, physical and spiritual bodies. We must fulfill the purpose for which we came into the earth plane, that is, to be again one with the Father, which is attained through the Christ Consciousness. Therefore, through the power of the Christ, who has walked the

[2]Gen. 1:3   [3]Gen. 6:2; see Gen. 4:16-17

path from the beginning, we will come to know ourselves to be ourselves, yet one with and part of, the whole, yet not the Whole. That is the purpose, that is the cause, of *Being*.

Time, Space and Patience

The Spirit of God in material understanding is Time, Space and Patience. While they are only literal terms to the consciousness of the finite mind, they are a part of experience in materiality and should be considered as attributes of Creative Force. In understanding time, we better understand God. No other concept can bring such a consciousness of unity as an inner flash of the universality of time.

Every day is the beginning and the ending of a new opportunity. Every opportunity has its beginning and end, thus making way for greater physical manifestation of spiritual ideals. Every new experience is another Garden of Eden into which we have moved. Every day is the awareness of the evening and the morning being the first day. To remain in Eden or to be driven out depends upon ourselves; as to how we use our power of choice. Every moment we are just beginning to live. We are never too old to begin, if we remember that in our weakness we may be strong in Christ.

God is reflected in our concept of space. In the vastness of space our self-conceit falters. We are humblest when gazing at the stars. We draw nearer to God in contemplation of the immensity of the universe.

The goodness and mercy of God are shown most in patience. To be patient is God-like; for patience is a spiritual force which may be given material expression through our attitude toward our fellow human beings. Jesus said that in patience we come to possess our souls. We become aware of the continuity of life as we are patient. As finite beings we can express no more God-like quality than patience.

Time, space and patience are three concepts which contain the keys to spiritual development in this three-dimensional plane. Without them fallen humanity is not aware of being away from God. They are the eye openers, the Voice of God speaking in the burning bush, "day unto day uttering speech, night unto night showing knowledge." (See Ps. 19:2.)

Using time and space and patience we measure everything,

physical, mental and spiritual. When we begin to catch a glimpse
of the fact that all space exists in time, that all time is one, that
all force is one, that all force is God, we will be getting back to the
Oneness of which Christ was speaking when He said that He
would be in the Father and we would be in Him. This realization
comes to us only in patience.

Self the Barrier

Selfishness is the influence which blocks our return to God
Consciousness.

We must begin to build up within ourselves that mind which
was in the Christ, if we would know God. The choice is ours. He
has set before us this day good and evil. He is "not willing that any
should perish,"[4] but that all should know the truth; "and ye shall
know the truth, and the truth shall make you free."[5]

Is God not the God of the heaven, the universe? Should He not
be God of the nation, the state, the home? What moves us to find
fault with our neighbor, to cause inharmonies in home, in the
state, in the nation? What are we doing in our daily conversations
and actions to express our recognition of the One Spirit? Are we
letting selfishness block the way, or are we being led by the Spirit
of Truth?

The Spirit of the Christ cannot abide in a selfish heart. We
drive Christ from our homes, from our churches, from our state—
yes, from our own consciousness when we seek self-glory.

It was the cause of the first turning away from God. It was the
first sin.

Experiences

"It was Christmas Eve. The day's work was done. I was tired,
so I lay down for a moment to reflect. I hadn't had much money
to spend for the things that generally go to make Christmas Day
happy. I began to look back on the day's work. In service I had
done my best to make others happy. I had tried to be unselfish.

"When I thought of myself again, I realized that my body was
entirely rested, although I had been lying down only a few
moments. Is it possible, I thought, that true rest comes from the
realization of a selfless life? If so, I had made the demonstration;
no great demonstration, to be sure, but one to me, that was the

[4]II Peter 3:9   [5]John 8:32

natural result of being selfless for one day."[6]

"During the first part of a spiritual discourse, which was a wonderful explanation of conditions of the world, I was following closely the questions that were being asked. Then, it seemed that I was up somewhere, high (unaware of being a person—just a 'consciousness'). I was looking down on a most beautiful, broad river, composed of flowing bubbles. It looked so smooth and almost musical—as the bubbles rolled on, around and over each other. I realized that the bubbles were PEOPLE! They, the bubbles, finally reached a place where they burst, and all seemed to be one. I thought 'It is the River of Life!' We, too, in the end will merge into the Whole; for we are one."[7]

Conclusion

We are constantly meeting that which we have measured unto others, as well as unto ourselves. The fruits we sow we must reap. If we disobey the laws pertaining to cleanliness, or the natural laws of nature, do we not meet the result in ourselves? Just so, it is with our mental and spiritual environment or association. To whom do we accredit these influences that are so much a part of our mental abilities and faculties if not to self's choice?

Let us know in whom we believe, and who is the author of our desires. Are our desires creative or destructive? "Father, let Thy desires be my desires. Let my desires, God, be Thy desires, in spirit and in truth," (262-60) should be our prayer. Thus we find grace, mercy, peace, and harmony becoming more and more a part of our experience. We love others, not merely because they love us, but because it brings harmony and hope into our own experience as we recognize God in our neighbor.

Our religion, our love for our fellow human beings, our love for our Creator should be a living experience, not just form. Truth, as mercy and grace, GROWS through use. As we manifest the fruits of the spirit in our dealings with our fellow humans, we fulfill that purpose for which we are called. We show forth the love we hold for our Maker by the manner in which we deal with our neighbor. God's love has manifested again and again in the earth showing us that by love, not hate and force, a soul may be brought to an awareness of its spiritual reality.

If we would be miserable, then let us think only of self. If we

[6]P.E.   [7]P.E.

would know happiness, then be a friend to someone. If we would know the love of God, then show love to those who seek, to those who condemn. Be joyous in the Lord, knowing that He is ever present when we seek His face. He is ever with us when we desire to be an emissary that others may know what it means to walk and talk with Him.

When we efface self and seek only to be led by His Spirit, then and only then may we hope to do our part in the scheme of redemption. Let us analyze our desires, our purposes, put away from our mind, our heart, our experience, those things that would make us afraid, and know that the true spirit of creative influence is WITHIN.

That which has a beginning must have an ending. Hence rebellion, selfishness, and hate, must be wiped away, and with them must go sorrow, tears and sadness. ONLY GOOD is everlasting. It is the Spirit of God that moved over the face of the earth, and gives this Spirit the charge concerning His own. Are we His own?

He has committed to us the keeping of His sheep, the tending of His lambs, until He comes and makes an accounting with each of us.

Where, O Where, will we be? (See 262-114.)

BIBLIOGRAPHY OF RECOMMENDED
PARALLEL MATERIAL

(Available directly from A.R.E. Press, 215 67th Street, Virginia Beach, VA 23451-2061; write for catalog.)

A Search for God, Book I
A Search for God, Book II
Experiments in a Search for God: The Edgar Cayce Path of Application
Experiments in Practical Spirituality
There Is a River (biography of Edgar Cayce)

The transcriptions of the original readings (from which the *Search for God* books were distilled) given to the first Study Group and Prayer Group are also available as companion texts:

Meditation, Part I (Prayer Group Readings), *Library Series,* Volume 2.
Study Group Readings (from which *A Search for God* text was compiled), *Library Series,* Volume 7.

EDGAR CAYCE'S A.R.E.

Who Was Edgar Cayce?
Twentieth Century Psychic and Medical Clairvoyant

Edgar Cayce (pronounced Kay-Cee, 1877-1945) has been called the "sleeping prophet," the "father of holistic medicine," and the most-documented psychic of the 20th century. For more than 40 years of his adult life, Cayce gave psychic "readings" to thousands of seekers while in an unconscious state, diagnosing illnesses and revealing lives lived in the past and prophecies yet to come. But who, exactly, was Edgar Cayce?

Cayce was born on a farm in Hopkinsville, Kentucky, in 1877, and his psychic abilities began to appear as early as his childhood. He was able to see and talk to his late grandfather's spirit, and often played with "imaginary friends" whom he said were spirits on the other side. He also displayed an uncanny ability to memorize the pages of a book simply by sleeping on it. These gifts labeled the young Cayce as strange, but all Cayce really wanted was to help others, especially children.

Later in life, Cayce would find that he had the ability to put himself into a sleep-like state by lying down on a couch, closing his eyes, and folding his hands over his stomach. In this state of relaxation and meditation, he was able to place his mind in contact with all time and space—the universal consciousness, also known as the super-conscious mind. From there, he could respond to questions as broad as, "What are the secrets of the universe?" and "What is my purpose in life?" to as specific as, "What can I do to help my arthritis?" and "How were the pyramids of Egypt built?" His responses to these questions came to be called "readings," and their insights offer practical help and advice to individuals even today.

The majority of Edgar Cayce's readings deal with holistic health and the treatment of illness. Yet, although best known for this material, the sleeping Cayce did not seem to be limited to concerns about the physical body. In fact, in their entirety, the readings discuss an astonishing 10,000 different topics. This vast array of subject matter can be narrowed down into a smaller group of topics that, when compiled together, deal with the following five categories: (1) Health-Related Information; (2) Philosophy and Reincarnation; (3) Dreams and Dream Interpretation; (4) ESP and Psychic Phenomena; and (5) Spiritual Growth, Meditation, and Prayer.

Learn more at EdgarCayce.org.

What Is A.R.E.?

Edgar Cayce founded the non-profit Association for Research and Enlightenment (A.R.E.) in 1931, to explore spirituality, holistic health, intuition, dream interpretation, psychic development, reincarnation, and ancient mysteries—all subjects that frequently came up in the more than 14,000 documented psychic readings given by Cayce.

The Mission of the A.R.E. is to help people transform their lives for the better, through research, education, and application of core concepts found in the Edgar Cayce readings and kindred materials that seek to manifest the love of God and all people and promote the purposefulness of life, the oneness of God, the spiritual nature of humankind, and the connection of body, mind, and spirit.

With an international headquarters in Virginia Beach, Va., a regional headquarters in Houston, regional representatives throughout the U.S., Edgar Cayce Centers in more than thirty countries, and individual members in more than seventy countries, the A.R.E. community is a global network of individuals.

A.R.E. conferences, international tours, camps for children and adults, regional activities, and study groups allow like-minded people to gather for educational and fellowship opportunities worldwide.

A.R.E. offers membership benefits and services that include a quarterly body-mind-spirit member magazine, *Venture Inward*, a member newsletter covering the major topics of the readings, and access to the entire set of readings in an exclusive online database.

Learn more at EdgarCayce.org.

EDGARCAYCE.ORG